SPOOKY

Spooky Appalachia

Also in the Spooky Series by S. E. Schlosser and Paul G. Hoffman

SPOOKY
Spooky Appalachia

Tales of Hauntings, Strange Happenings,
and Other Local Lore

RETOLD BY S. E. SCHLOSSER

ILLUSTRATED BY PAUL G. HOFFMAN

Globe
Pequot

ESSEX, CONNECTICUT

Globe Pequot

An imprint of Globe Pequot, the trade division of
The Rowman & Littlefield Publishing Group, Inc.
4501 Forbes Blvd., Ste. 200
Lanham, MD 20706
www.rowman.com

Distributed by NATIONAL BOOK NETWORK

British Library Cataloguing in Publication Information available

Library of Congress Cataloging-in-Publication Data

Names: Schlosser, S. E., author.
Title: Spooky Appalachia : tales of hauntings, strange happenings, and other
  local lore / retold by S.E. Schlosser ; illustrated by Paul Hoffman.
Description: Essex, Connecticut : Globe Pequot, [2024] | Includes
  bibliographical references.
Identifiers: LCCN 2024004334 (print) | LCCN 2024004335 (ebook) |
  ISBN 9781493085712 (paperback) | ISBN 9781493085729 (epub)
Subjects: LCSH: Ghost stories, American—Appalachian Region. | Ghosts—
  Appalachian Region. | Haunted places—Appalachian Region. | Appalachian
  Region.
Classification: LCC BF1472.U6 S2925 2024 (print) | LCC BF1472.U6
  (ebook) | DDC 133.10974—dc23/eng/20240416
LC record available at https://lccn.loc.gov/2024004334
LC ebook record available at https://lccn.loc.gov/2024004335

For my family: David, Dena, Tim, Arlene, Hannah, Seth, Theo, Rory, Emma, Nathan, Ben, Karen, Davey, Deb, Gabe, Clare, Jack, and Chris.

For my friends: Jessica, Peter, Evelyn, Eleanor, and Grace.

For Sandy Laws and the staff at the Archives of Appalachia. Thank you so much for your help.

For Greta Schmitz, Paul Hoffman, and the staff at Globe Pequot. Thanks for all you do!

Contents

SPOOKY SITES . . .

①	Pittsburgh, PA	⑯	Cortland County, NY
②	Binghampton, NY	⑰	Wilkes Barre, PA
③	Cincinnati, OH	⑱	Chillicothe, OH
④	Hagerstown, MD	⑲	Charleston, WV
⑤	Raleigh County, WV	⑳	Point Pleasant, WV
⑥	Bedford County, VA	㉑	Wise County, VA
⑦	Ashland, KY	㉒	Swain County, NC
⑧	Asheville, NC	㉓	Great Smoky Mountains National Park, NC
⑨	Knoxville, TN	㉔	Chilhowee Mountain, TN
⑩	Adams, TN	㉕	Chattanooga, TN
⑪	Greenville, SC	㉖	Cumberland Gap, KY
⑫	Chatsworth, GA	㉗	Spartanburg County, SC
⑬	Atlanta, GA	㉘	Gainesville, GA
⑭	Birmingham, AL	㉙	Wheeler National Wildlife Refuge, AL
⑮	Lee County, MS	㉚	Houston, MS

AND WHERE TO FIND THEM

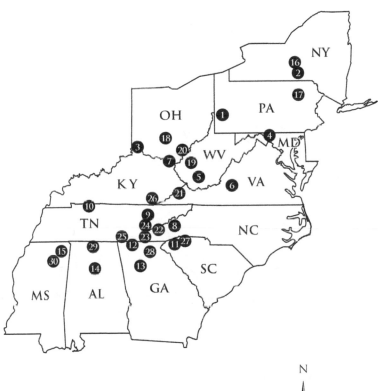

Introduction

When I moved to the Blue Ridge Mountains of Appalachia a few years ago, I did not realize that I had chosen to live in one of the most haunted regions in the United States. I was too busy finding the grocery store and getting my new house painted to pay attention to apparitions.

My first inkling came when I joined the local pool club and learned that the lifeguards were being haunted by the ghost of a little boy who liked to play pranks on them in the pool house after hours. The pool house was a modernized colonial-era stable, and the little specter was believed to have perished there in the 1700s. Also appearing in this very modern setting was a phantom woman in colonial working garb. She was said to be the former nanny of the little boy. All summer long, there were happy splashes and shouts without the clubhouse, and ghostly giggles and slamming doors within.

Things just got spookier from there. With Appomattox courthouse and its ghostly soldiers a few miles down the road and Thomas Jefferson's Poplar Forest—complete with the former president's apparition still in residence—just around the corner, paranormal manifestations were taken for granted around here. The local Civil War graveyard was so haunted that many life-long residents refused to set foot in it, day or night.

I quickly discovered the Blue Ridge Parkway just a few miles from my home. A short drive along this famous byway brought me to an infamous gap where a ghost hound haunts the place where his owner was murdered. ("The Black Dog") In the town below, the apparition of a mad witch is rumored to lurk in the woods, bringing death and destruction to all who encounter her.

Driving north to visit relatives, I often found myself in coal country, where musical miners return from the dead ("The Minstrel"), the sound of a clock ticking warns of impending doom ("The Death Watch"), and a Vampire Hermit lurks in the back woods.

When I headed south to visit friends, I passed Wise County, where a household was once bewitched by a neighbor seeking revenge, ("The Witch's Shoulder") as well as the Cumberland Gap, where colonial settlers were said to have sold their souls in exchange for special powers ("The Devil's Book").

A weekend trip to the Smoky Mountains of Tennessee found me hiking the same trails as the ancient stone giant called Spear-Finger and driving slowly along the road where a worker once encountered a Boojum in the vicinity of Chattanooga ("Boojum"). (Alas, Bigfoot was too busy to hitch a ride with me that day.)

And on a recent family vacation, my sister, nephew, and I visited a natural bridge where the spirit of a native chief lingered, watching over his land. Just another day in the life in Appalachia, apparently.

So, readers, take note: If you stop at an abandoned house anywhere in Appalachia, do not—I beg you—Wait Until Emmett Comes. You have been warned.

Happy Hauntings!

—Sandy Schlosser

PART ONE
Ghost Stories

1

Hot Steel

His lame leg prevented him from serving in the army when World War II broke out in Europe. That didn't stop him from trying to help out in any way he could. For decades, his family had worked a farm just outside Pittsburgh. One day shortly after the United States joined the war, the farmer packed a satchel full of clothes and went to town to find a job in Jones and Laughlin Steel Corporation's Number 2 Shop at the Southside steel mill complex. Pittsburgh had become the Arsenal of Democracy for World War II, producing steel not just for America, but also for its allies, and he wanted to be a part of the effort.

The farmer found it difficult to adjust to his new life. The pollution was terrible. Thick black smoke choked the skies, forcing people to drive their cars with headlights on at noon in order to see where they were going. Chemicals from the factories spewed into the river, where they mixed with untreated human waste. There were dead fish everywhere, and the farmer was appalled when he discovered that the river water was being pumped back into the city untreated as drinking water for homes and businesses.

HOT STEEL

Worst to his mind was the large number of people crammed into his community. The farmer was almost never alone: Mothers, fathers, children, single workers, old folks, and the young were everywhere he turned. They got on his nerves after the open spaces and sparse neighborhood in the farmlands of his home. He hated living in ill-housed, overworked, disorganized, and generally squalid Pittsburgh. Folks called it "Hell with the Lid Off," and he heartily agreed with their sentiments. Still, he was doing his bit for the country, and that helped soothe his pride, which was regularly hurt by the limitations of his lame leg.

The farmer was put to work in the melt shop and soon learned to be very careful around the furnace and the ladles full of molten steel. The other workers often spoke about Joe Macarac, the ultimate steel hero of folklore whose exploits were akin to those of Paul Bunyan. According to the workers, Macarac not only drank hot steel for soup, he could also scoop it up in his bare hands and form it into horseshoes and cannonballs. Macarac once caught a falling ladle full of molten steel with his bare hands, easing it safely to the ground and saving the lives of his crew. This piece of folklore comforted the men, the farmer knew, since every worker feared what would happen if the chains holding the ladles full of molten steel ever broke while they passed overhead. Burning to death in molten steel might be a quick demise, but it would be agonizing.

This was the reason that the tale of the ghost in the steel mill, while complete fiction in the farmer's opinion, was still heart-wrenching and horrible. Apparently, a man named Jim Grabowski tripped over a rigger hose back in 1922 and fell into a ladle of hot steel. His body was immediately liquefied; there was nothing left for his family to bury save for a small nugget of steel that was skimmed from the tainted ladle before its contents were dumped into a vacant lot. From that day onward, the workers said that Jim's ghost clanked its way around 2 Shop at night, searching for his dead body. Some men claimed to have heard the ghost screaming in agony as he relived his final moments. The screams were shortly followed by the maniacal laughter of the ghost, whose mind had gone mad with the pain of his death.

The farmer was not afraid of the ghost. He thought the story was as much a tall tale as the exploits of Joe Macarac. When other men shied away from night work in the melt shop, he volunteered to take their shifts. He liked the extra money this earned him, and soon his reputation for fearlessness and his scorn for the ghost of Jim Grabowski were the talk of the mill.

There came an evening when the farmer found himself alone on the furnace floor. It was the slow time between shifts, and by rights he should already be on his way home. However, he had stayed behind for a moment to complete a small task, and he hummed contentedly to himself as he bent over his work. He gradually became aware of a muffled sound coming from somewhere to his left. He ignored it, since the mechanized processes all around him often made strange sounds.

The sound grew louder, and the farmer finally looked up from his labors to see a glowing white mist gathering in the air a few yards away from where he stood. The mist emitted a faint rapping noise, which slowly clarified into the steady thud of approaching footsteps.

The farmer gasped, goose bumps forming on his arms in spite of the heat from the furnace. He watched with unblinking eyes as the mist solidified into the glowing figure of a workman making his rounds. Suddenly, the man tripped and fell downward in slow motion toward a shimmering ladle full of steaming molten steel. The phantom workman's body plunged into the hot liquid, and he tried in vain to grab the sides of the ladle and pull himself out, unwilling to believe that he was doomed. Then, his body liquefying and his face hideously twisted with pain, the ghostly workman screamed desperately for someone to save him as he sank downward into the red-hot ladle. With a final, hair-raising shriek, the apparition disappeared.

The farmer's own scream of sheer terror was so loud that it cut through the voice of the phantom, echoing and reechoing through the furnace room. Dropping his tools as if he himself were burning up, the farmer raced for the exit as fast as his lame leg would take him, the gut-wrenching sound of maniacal laughter behind him.

He ran all the way home, packed his satchel, and set out at once for his home. The farmer stopped just long enough to inform his boss that he was quitting, then limped down the smoke-filled roads toward the outskirts of town, thumbing for a lift whenever he saw a pair of headlights pierce the smoggy dawn. He never looked back.

The farmer spent the rest of the war growing crops and providing food for those who labored in the steel mills. He always sent a representative into Pittsburgh with his produce rather than venture into that terrible, phantom-filled city again. Once was enough.

2

Fifty Cents

BINGHAMTON, NY

The young couple departed much later than they expected from their cousin's house. They were still miles from home when dusk fell over the narrow, windy road they traveled. The horses were tired, the night was chilly, and there was no inn anywhere in sight. The husband clicked his tongue thoughtfully, a sure sign that he was getting worried. His young wife laid a hand on his arm and suggested that they seek out a house and ask for shelter for the night. Her husband considered this proposal for a moment, then smiled and acquiesced. As they traveled the long, bumpy road, they started watching for a house.

It was the husband who spied a light through the trees just when his wife had resigned herself to a cold night spent in a parked carriage. He turned their horse onto a narrow dirt road leading up a hill. A pleasant little house stood at the crest. The light was shining cheerfully from the windows, illuminating a pretty, well-kept yard.

Their carriage was spotted as they drove up the hill, and an old man and his wife met the couple at the door. The old folks were in nightclothes and had obviously been about to go to bed, but their welcome was warm. The elderly couple

FIFTY CENTS

introduced themselves as Mr. and Mrs. Brown. The old wife took the young woman by the arm, tutting briskly over her cold hands.

"You'll catch your death out in this cold, damp air," Mrs. Brown exclaimed. "Papa, throw some more wood on the fire."

She whisked the young folks inside the cozy house and settled them into comfortable chairs close to the fireplace before the young husband could explain the reason for their unexpected visit.

As old man Brown built up the fire, the young man asked if they might rent a room for the night, since there was no inn nearby and they were still many miles from home.

"Rent? Don't be ridiculous," exclaimed Mrs. Brown. "You must be our guests!" She ignored the young couple's protests and bustled out of the room to get them some hot food. Feeling overwhelmed by such kindness, the young man and his pretty wife supped on the good meat and cakes placed before them and chatted merrily with their host and his wife.

After the impromptu dinner, old man Brown and his wife escorted the weary couple to their room. As they parted for the night, the young husband once again volunteered to pay for their lodgings. Mrs. Brown stiffened and shook her head reproachfully at the young man, and her husband said: "Nay, lad, 'tis but a small service we offer you. Keep your money and buy something pretty for your young lady."

The travelers woke early and tiptoed out of the cozy house. The young husband hesitated a moment, and then left a shiny fifty-cent coin in the center of the kitchen table where the old couple could not miss it. Then he hitched up their horse, and they went on their way. After several miles, they came to Binghamton. Spotting an inn, they went inside and purchased breakfast.

The innkeeper was a jolly fellow who came over to talk to them as they ate. When the husband mentioned the nice old couple who had given them lodging the previous night, the innkeeper turned pale.

"Where did you say that house was?" the innkeeper asked. The husband described the location in detail.

"You must be mistaken," said the innkeeper. "I know that place. That house was destroyed three years ago in a fire that killed the entire Brown family."

"I don't believe it," the husband said flatly. "Mr. and Mrs. Brown were alive and well last night."

After debating the matter for a few minutes, the couple and the innkeeper drove their carriage back out of town toward the old Brown place. The ground was quickly covered in bright sunshine, and the wife soon recognized the place where they had turned off the main road the night before. To her surprise, the narrow lane was overgrown with weeds, and dead branches crackled under the carriage wheels as they turned into it. She glanced uneasily at her husband and saw that he was equally disturbed. The track had not looked this way when they left earlier that morning. The carriage climbed the hill to the crest, and as they entered the yard, they saw a burned-out shell of a house that had obviously not sheltered anyone for a long time.

"This cannot be right," the wife exclaimed, climbing down out of the carriage and walking toward the blackened ruin.

"This is the Brown place," the innkeeper said.

"This is not where we stayed last evening," the husband insisted, slipping from the driver's seat to join the innkeeper on the ground. "I must have mistaken the direction."

And then the wife gave a terrified scream and swayed. Her husband leapt forward and caught her in his arms as she crumbled to the ground in a dead faint. Searching for the cause of her fright, the husband looked into the ruins and saw a burnt table with a shiny fifty-cent piece lying in the center, just where he had left it.

3

Marrying a Ghost

CINCINNATI

My wife, who is a strong believer in spiritualism, was eager to read, one frosty morning in late September, that the famed spiritualistic medium Mrs. Fairchild would be coming to Cincinnati in October.

"You should invite her to supper," I said at once, knowing that such an invitation would please my wife. Her face lit up and I got an excited kiss on the cheek before she went to her morning room to write to Mrs. Fairchild. Our supper invitation was eagerly accepted, and on the given evening, Mrs. Fairchild presented herself at our front door. The supper talk ranged far and wide, covering spirit guides and ectoplasm and apports, among other things. Then Mrs. Fairchild described an unusual case that would have its culmination right here in Cincinnati. Her story was as follows.

During her travels, Mrs. Fairchild was approached by a British expatriate from Birmingham who was residing in the United States. Mr. Charles Thorp was a wealthy bachelor who lost the sweetheart of his youth to illness before they could be married. After forty years, he was still faithful to her memory and sought to reconnect with her spirit via a medium. Mrs. Fairchild

MARRYING A GHOST

granted him a sitting and was able to materialize the spirit of the young woman, to the great joy of her former betrothed.

From that day onward, Mr. Thorp followed Mrs. Fairchild from city to city. He paid handsomely for sittings in which he became reacquainted with his deceased beloved, courting her again via the medium. After a dozen sittings in a dozen cities, Mr. Thorp made an unusual request. He wanted to marry his deceased sweetheart. He had proposed during a séance and she had accepted his suit. He wanted Mrs. Fairchild to arrange the ceremony for them. Mrs. Fairchild was startled. This was a new situation for her and one that—should it succeed—would push forward the boundaries of spiritualism. Mrs. Fairchild was intrigued and consented to put her powers of mediumship to the test. She would gain much fame if it could be achieved.

"And so," she concluded her story over the dessert course, "Mr. Thorp has come here to Cincinnati, where I will call forth the spirit of his beloved so they can be married in spirit and in truth, a state sadly denied them when they were young."

My wife's eyes were shining with excitement. "When will the wedding take place?" she asked.

"Tomorrow," Mrs. Fairchild revealed. "Right here on Seventh Street."

Seeing our interest, she invited us to be present for the ghostly ceremony, and we eagerly consented. It was the most singular social invitation we'd ever received.

"How romantic," my wife sighed sentimentally after the famed Mrs. Fairchild had departed. "To think, Mr. Thorp will be united at last with his beloved."

"Not much of a bargain," I said gruffly, donning my nightshirt. "It's pretty hard to cuddle a spirit."

I slipped my arms around my spouse and gave her a kiss on the cheek. She giggled and kissed me back.

We arrived at the house at 8 p.m. on the night of the ghost wedding and found the parlor filled with flowers. Mr. Thorp had arrived in Cincinnati the evening prior and made all the arrangements for the ceremony. The guests were few, less than a dozen, but they were all prominent citizens of this city. The bridegroom arrived at 8:30 p.m. I liked him at once. Mr. Thorp was a stately man of medium build. He had intelligent eyes and a handsome gray beard that looked snow-white against his black wedding coat. He wore a single white flower in his buttonhole. Introductions were made and soon everyone was talking and laughing with the ease of old friends. Mr. Thorp might have lived among us for years, so well did the stately bachelor fit into our little gathering.

Meanwhile, Mrs. Fairchild and the servants were preparing the wedding chamber. The spirit cabinet was set up in one corner and all ceremonial preparations made while we mingled. Finally, the famous medium called us into the flower-strewn chamber. The pollen made me sneeze, and I buried my nose in a handkerchief while my wife found us seats near the medium's cabinet. Mr. Thorp took the bridegroom's place at the front and Mrs. Fairchild stood beside the spirit cabinet.

The room grew still and silent as the servants lowered the lights. We sat in heavy darkness, and my wife groped for my hand. I felt her trembling and squeezed her long fingers comfortingly, wondering what would happen. As my eyes adjusted to the darkness, I could make out Mr. Thorp's silhouetted figure, his gray-white beard showing lighter than the objects around him.

One silent minute stretched into two as we gazed at the black shape of the cabinet. I wondered if our bridegroom was doomed to a second disappointment. Then a rustling sound ran through the room, like the swish of a curtain being drawn. The cabinet door swung open of its own accord.

"She comes," murmured Mrs. Fairchild.

A phosphorescent ball emerged through the cabinet door and floated toward Mr. Thorp, illuminating his handsome face and brightening his eyes. He looked ghostly himself in that strange light, and I shivered a bit, hoping this evening would have a happy ending. What if marrying a ghost meant you had to become a ghost yourself? The unsettling thought hadn't occurred to me before. Nervously, I shook it away.

The light floated to Mr. Thorp's right and a young woman in a white gown materialized at his side. She was as pale as death, but beautiful still. There was a smile on her white lips, which was echoed by the smile on the face of her (I hoped) still-living bridegroom.

The air in the room had dropped ten degrees as the bride manifested herself, and it continued to plummet as a second glowing figure appeared in the place where the holy priest usually stood. I was not expecting a spirit minister, and neither were the other guests, judging by the susurration of surprised murmurs that flowed through the observers. Mrs. Fairchild was the only one who did not appear disconcerted by this second ghostly presence.

To my surprise, the ministering spirit spoke the words of the ceremony aloud, starting with the traditional phrases used at my own wedding. Mr. Thorp said his vows in a strong voice, and the bride's voice answered him, soft and sweet. My wife's fingers tightened on my own, and she sighed with pleasure when the minister pronounced the couple husband and wife. The phantom minister raised his hands in benediction over the married pair. Mr. Thorp leaned forward to kiss his new wife. Then minister and bride slowly vanished away, leaving the room in darkness.

I swallowed, afraid I might cry and embarrass myself. How sad to make your beloved sweetheart your wife only to have her vanish before your eyes. I blew my nose on my handkerchief. Beside me, my wife was dabbing her eyes with her much daintier handkerchief.

There were many wet eyes among the watchers when the lights came up. But Mr. Thorp (still alive, thank goodness) looked as proud and happy as any other bridegroom. He wrung Mrs. Fairchild's hand and accepted our congratulations with satisfaction.

I looked him in the eye when we shook hands and he saw the question in mine.

"I know it's sad that we can't be together here on earth," he said to me. "But at least she's mine now for all eternity, and she'll be waiting for me at heaven's gate. I can feel her presence, even if I can't see her. I'm satisfied."

I wasn't. As we toasted the happy bridegroom and congratulated the skillful medium who made his happiness possible, I mulled over his words. I watched my wife, chatting with friends across the room. Would I be satisfied if she wasn't there to greet me every morning? I didn't think so.

The evening drew to a close. We thanked Mrs. Fairchild and our hosts, and I escorted my wife outside.

"What were you thinking about during the reception?" she asked, taking my hand as we strolled down Seventh Street. "You looked sad."

"I was just wondering about Mr. Thorp's future with his ghostly bride," I replied.

"Probably not much of a future there," she conceded. "Still, I am glad we attended the ceremony. It was the most remarkable spiritualist demonstration I've ever witnessed. I'm sure it was a true manifestation of both the bride and the minister. Mrs. Fairchild is obviously a very gifted medium . . . " Her voice trailed off.

"But?" I prompted when she didn't finish her thought.

"But I thought my heart would break when the bride vanished at the end of the ceremony," my wife confessed.

"It certainly made me appreciate my own life," I said. "A man with a ghost for his bride is not as lucky as me."

"That would have been true even if Mr. Thorp had married a living bride," my wife said archly.

I grinned and kissed her right there in the street. "Good point," I said and escorted her up the front stairs of our comfortable home on Seventh Street.

As my wife bustled through the door, I paused and looked back along the street. I wondered how Mr. Thorp would feel when he entered his empty bedchamber that evening. Then I wondered if his ghost bride would manifest in his room in the middle of the night. I shivered at the thought. I went inside my warm house and firmly locked the door against all spiritual manifestations.

4

Jinks

HAGERSTOWN, MD

On my second night home after mustering out from my company at the end of the Civil War, I woke up shivering in the sudden cold, wondering why the summer night felt so chilly. I rolled over and found myself looking at a glowing figure glaring at me from the foot of the bed. I was never so scared in my whole life. My body came all-over goose bumps and my hair positively stood on end. Gathering my courage, I exclaimed: "Who are you?"

"Name's Jinks," the specter said in a husky tone with an odd echo to it that made the flesh creep. "I'm the ghost of the rebel soldier you picked off in the battle of Bull Run."

My mind raced back to that fateful day. I'd picked off more than one rebel during that horror. Which one was this? Then I had it. "Are you the chap that hid behind the old log? The one who kept ducking down whenever I took aim? I didn't think I hit you."

"You sure did, seeing as I've been a ghost ever since that day," the specter growled. "I'm here to demand reparation."

JINKS

"Reparation?" I said indignantly, sitting up and hugging my knees to my chest. "What do you mean reparation? We faced off in a battle. It was a fair fight. I can't bring you back to life."

"You can't," Jinks said in sepulchral tones. "But there's my widow to consider. I looked in on her yesterday and she's having a hard time getting along. You must hunt her up and tell her to dig the little farm for coal."

My ears perked up. Coal? There was good money to be had in coal. "How do you know there's coal there?" I asked skeptically.

The glowing figure gave an eerie smile. "It is my province to know things denied to you mortals. Now, will you go?"

I considered thoughtfully. I didn't much like my current job, and a potentially rich widow sounded mighty tempting. I loved my mother, but once a fellow has been living on his own, he really prefers his own place. "Where is your widow living now?" I asked.

"It's not far," said the ghost of Mr. Jinks. He gave very specific directions to a place near Hagerstown, Maryland. I listened intently and started calculating the cost of taking such a trip. A high sum.

"When can you start?" growled the specter.

"I'll head south tomorrow. I should see your widow in about ten days," I replied. "Do you have a message you wish to send?"

Jinks sat himself down on the bed—or tried too. He sank too deeply into the mattress. "No message," he said emphatically. "As a ghost, I can only appear to the person who caused my death. If I send a message to Melinda through you, she'll know you killed me and boy howdy will you get it. Still, I thought lots of her, and she just worshiped me." He gave a gusty sigh that made the hairs on my neck prickle.

How interesting. So, Jinks and his wife didn't get along when he was still in the land of the living. "Why didn't you agree?" I asked curiously.

"Melinda was very industrious," Jinks said. "She was always working. And I was born tired. She never understood that. Come to think of it, you may have done me a good turn at Bull Run. Now I don't have to hustle for anything to eat, the heat doesn't bother me, and I can rest whenever I like. When Melinda is provided for, I promise I'll stop haunting you. Just keep it a dead secret that you killed me. Melinda loved me to desperation despite everything and she'd kill you if she knew you done me in and send your ghost a-wandering like mine."

"I'll make sure your widow is provided for," I said vaguely. "And I accept your promise to stop haunting me when I do."

Jinks nodded several times and then spiraled away until the room was dark once more.

I left promptly the next morning and made my way slowly south. I'd recently taken on the job of selling patent washing machines, and my new employers didn't care where I sold them, so when I told them I was heading to Maryland, they wished me a good journey and that was that. So, I worked my way south with my merchandise, heading toward poor, lonely Widow Jinks . . . and the coal in her backyard.

During my journey south, if the householders permitted it, I would bring the washing machine inside and wash out a few pieces of their linen to show them how it worked. We shared tips on the best methods of stain removal and how to get a collar good and stiff. I became quite an expert in the art of washing.

All of this was good practice for my encounter with Widow Jinks. My plan was to ask Mrs. Jinks to board at her place while I sold my washer to the folks in the surrounding county, and I'd ingratiate myself by helping her with the laundry on washday. I figured I had to feel my way carefully before mentioning a possible coal field. Otherwise, she'd call me a scallywag and send me packing.

Exactly ten days later, I reached the Jinks place in Maryland. I knocked on the door, and it was opened by an old woman. My heart plummeted. I'd been expecting a young lady. The ghost of Mr. Jinks hadn't looked old. But apparently, I'd assumed wrong. Still, I'd given my word to the specter that I'd help his widow, so I'd stick with the plan.

"Is this Mrs. Jinks?" I asked politely.

"Law, no," the old lady smiled. "I'm Mrs. Friedman that lives with her now that her no-good husband has passed. Step inside and rest a bit while we wait for Melinda. She's running some errands and should be along shortly."

The front room was neat and clean, but there wasn't much furniture. The pieces were rather threadbare and worn, just as I expected from what the ghost of Jinks told me. Mrs. Friedman and I hit it off splendidly. She quickly confided in me that Melinda Jinks was far better off without her husband, who she described as the most shiftless and laziest man that ever lived.

Mrs. Friedman broke off suddenly and gestured toward the window. "Here comes Melinda now," she said with a fond smile. I gazed through the glass at a lovely dark-haired woman with bright eyes and a resolute chin. She looked like she wouldn't take any nonsense from a lazy husband, and I liked her the better for it. In fact, I was pretty taken with the Widow Jinks right from the start. She listened intently to Mrs. Friedman's introduction, and her attention sharpened further when I said: "I had the honor of being connected with the late Mr. Jinks in the late war. It was his earnest desire, if he was killed, that I should carry a message of his undying affection for you. It has been impossible for me to reach you until now, but please rest assured I came as quickly as I could."

"Thank you very much for your kindness, Mr. Wilkins," Widow Jinks said. "I am glad to meet someone who knew William during the war."

I winced inwardly at her kind words and felt like a fraud. Still, this was what the ghost of Jinks wanted me to do.

Oddly, she did not ask for further particulars about her husband, and I didn't pursue the matter. Instead, I described the business that brought me to this part of the country and asked if she would be willing to board me while I worked. Widow Jinks said she'd take me on, and though she didn't say so, I received the impression she and Mrs. Friedman were glad of the extra income.

On my first night at the cottage, I had a spectral visitor. Jinks appeared at the foot of my bed in his Confederate uniform. I rubbed my eyes sleepily and growled: "What now? I'm here like you asked me to be. Can't you let me sleep in peace?"

"I just wanted to know how you are coming on," the ghost grumbled.

"Well enough so far," I said, sitting up with a sigh. "But it's going to be a slow business breaking the news of the coal field to her."

"Why is that?" asked William Jinks suspiciously.

"Because she's got to have faith in me, or she'll think I'm telling tall tales," I replied. "If she doesn't believe me, she won't go looking for the coal and your haunting will be in vain."

The specter was much struck by my words. "That's true. Melinda is no pushover. Still, you should hurry it up as fast as you can. Melinda hates to have a man bothering about the place." With that piece of advice, the ghost vanished.

Well, she certainly didn't care to have you hanging about, I thought as I rolled over and went back to sleep.

The next few weeks were the happiest I'd ever lived. I had wonderful luck selling my patent washing machines. When I wasn't meeting friendly people and making their lives a little bit better, I was doing odd jobs around the house to earn my keep. My mother taught me to make myself useful and that's just what I did. I repaired the fence, fixed the leaking roof, built a shed, chopped firewood, and fixed Mrs. Friedman's spinning wheel. And so forth.

In the evenings, I'd sit with the ladies on the little front porch and tell them lighthearted stories from my days as a soldier. We laughed heartily at some of the antics the men got up to between battles. Widow Jinks and Mrs. Friedman countered with little stories about the people and animals living in the region, and their tales were equally interesting to me.

The disclosure of the coal field had completely slipped my mind until a month to the day after my arrival, when the ghost of Mr. Jinks appeared once again in my room.

"What is the meaning of this delay," the specter demanded. He was so angry that blue sparks shot out of his glowing body in all directions.

"Relax, Jinks," I said uneasily. The ghost was quite disconcerting. For the first time, I wondered if Jinks could harm me if I didn't obey his request. "I am going to tell her tomorrow."

"See that you do," the ghost said with a red-eyed glare. "Or I'll run you off the place."

"Hogwash," I said.

I decided the ghost was more bluster than business. Still, I'd given my word. It was time to act. And once my part of the bargain was fulfilled, the ghost couldn't haunt me anymore. Jinks had given me his promise.

The next evening, I found Widow Jinks alone on the porch. "Mrs. Friedman has gone to the village," she explained.

"I'm glad I caught you alone," I said, sitting down on the steps at her feet. "I've been wishing to tell you something. I've made a discovery while working around your place, and it's something I can tell only to you."

Mrs. Jinks clasped her hands tightly together and I felt her gaze on me. Her eyes were dark and luminous in the moonlight.

"I think there is coal on this land, right underneath your house," I said, addressing the stick in my hand instead of the lovely woman beside me. "If this is true, you stand to become a wealthy woman. If you don't have the means to make the investigation yourself, I am happy to advance you whatever capital you need as a partial share in the mine, should coal be found." I reddened and added: "You wouldn't have to pay me back if it's a false alarm. It's just what anyone speculating on coal would do in my place."

Melinda Jinks straightened herself, and it seemed as if she was disappointed somehow. I turned to look at her. "How do you know there is coal here?" she asked. Her voice was cool, and I'd never heard that tone from her before. My heart sank.

"Your husband told me his suspicions about it. I wanted to make sure his idea was correct before telling you. I didn't want to raise false hopes," I explained.

"You are very kind," the Widow Jinks said, still in that cool tone. "I'll go in now and think it over."

She rose and it felt like a wall had been erected between us. I was devastated. I reached out suddenly and caught her hand. She paused and looked down at me.

"I've discovered something else," I said in a husky voice. "But I am afraid to tell you."

Melinda Jinks slowly sank down into her chair. Her eyes were suddenly warm, and my heart started to pound against my ribs. She didn't speak, but I could tell she wanted me to continue.

"I've discovered that you are the one woman in the world for me," I said. "But how can I ask you to marry me when you will be rich, and I am just a poor soldier who sells washing machines."

Melinda's eyes told me what she thought of that nonsense.

"Will you have me?" I asked humbly.

She smiled and I knelt on the top step and took her in my arms.

"We don't have to do anything about the coal field," I told her after our first kiss. "I'll take you to meet my family, and then settle anywhere you like. I can earn a good living selling washing machines."

"Pshaw," said my lady. "Why would we ignore the coal field? It will be money for our children and grandchildren."

"And Mrs. Friedman will live with us. She'll like having children underfoot," I continued. "I suggest we have a new house built in the town while I take you to meet my family. After that, if you wish we can begin work on the coal field."

Melinda gave me another kiss to confirm our plan.

"I confess I feel much better now that you know about the coal," I said. "I feel like Jinks can rest in peace now that you are taken care of."

"Mr. Jinks," Melinda said crisply, "Was always very good at resting. You, on the other hand, are very good at working. Which is why I will have you or none."

This declaration earned her a third kiss.

I waited several hours after I retired for the ghost to arrive. Jinks swirled into being in a flash of blue light at the foot of my bed and eyed me expectantly. "Did you tell her?" he demanded eagerly.

"I told her," I confirmed. "She is very happy."

The ghost of Mr. Jinks rubbed his hands with glee. "That's good, that's good," he cried. "I'm obliged to you for your trouble, though frankly I don't see how you could have done much less. Still, a promise is a promise. I'll stop haunting you now. You are free to go back North."

"And what are you going to do?" I asked, curious about how a ghost occupied itself once its earthly mission was complete.

"Me? "I'll keep Melinda company from now on," said William Jinks. "She won't be able to see me, of course, but I'm sure it will gladden her lonely heart to feel my presence in this house. Now, how soon can you leave? I don't wish to be inhospitable, but this house is mine and I've decided to live here permanently. The sooner you get away, the better."

I was nettled by his obvious desire to be rid of me. After all, I'd done him a favor. "I am going as soon as I can get married," I told him. "In about two days' time."

"Married?" said the ghost. "Well, well. So, you found yourself a bride during your stay here! I only hope that you get as devoted a wife as my Melinda."

"I am quite sure I have," I said briskly. "And my bride and I will be happy to leave you in possession of these premises."

William Jinks eyed me suspiciously. "Who'd you say you were going to marry?" he asked.

"Melinda Jinks," I said.

The ghost of Mr. Jinks reared up in shock and started sparking blue flames from every part of his body. He was furious and I could tell he wanted to kill me right there and then. But he'd promised to stop haunting me if I did as he bade me, and I knew he couldn't touch me. The flaming ghost lunged toward me, arms outstretched to grab and strangle. I held my ground; certain that I was right. Just before Jinks reached me, he hit a wall of pure white energy that flung him backward with such force that he vanished through the far wall.

"Good riddance," I said in satisfaction.

That was the last time I saw the ghost of Mr. Jinks.

5

The Death Watch

Jim Kelly had dreaded this day for weeks. It was the first day of his new job, but it was a job he knew well. For fourteen years he had managed to escape the everlasting darkness, the dangers, the long climbs, and the narrow crawl spaces of the coal mines. Jim had hated the life of a coal miner. But with seven children to feed, he felt he had no choice but to return.

When Jim was thirteen his mother was widowed, and he went to work in a coal mine to help support his struggling family. But when Jim turned sixteen, his mother remarried a wealthy man. His new stepfather found Jim a place as a clerk in a store when he learned how Jim felt about mining.

Jim had done well at the store. He'd married his sweetheart Margaret when he was eighteen. They'd had seven children and bought a nice house in town, far away from the horrors of the coal mine. But then disaster struck in the form of a terrible fire that wiped out the entire town, leaving Jim without a home or a job.

Jim's youngest sister, Susan, took his family in until they could find another place to live, and Jeff, Jim's brother-in-law, got Jim a job working with him in the coal mine. Jim said the

THE DEATH WATCH

family was grateful to have a roof over their heads; still, he hated going back to mining. Margaret insisted it was only temporary. The town would be rebuilt, and Jim could go back to the store. Jim clung to that hope as he followed Jeff down the ladder into the darkness of the mine.

Jim had lost none of his mining skills, and he quickly settled into the daily routine. He stayed with Jeff for the first few days, working a coal seam, stooped over because the shaft was only five feet tall. All day they stood ankle deep in water, which constantly dripped from the ceiling. The conditions in this mine were just as miserable as in the mine where Jim had worked as a boy. But Jeff was a good companion, and he made that first week bearable with his friendly conversation. On the first day, Jeff told Jim the story of the death watch.

"Old Ted Miller was a bad one," Jeff said while they were taking a lunch break in the only dry space in the shaft they were working. "We always suspected he was stealing from the mine, but we never knew for sure until one day he was buried alive by a pillar of coal he was robbing. We dug his body out, but we couldn't find his watch. He used to keep it hanging on a timber in the heading, but he must have had it with him on the day he died because although we could hear it ticking away, we never could find it."

Jeff took a drink and continued. "After a few days, the ticking stopped, and we thought no more of it. Until the day that Amos and Joshua heard the sound of a watch ticking in their seam. They were working a small seam—about twenty-eight inches wide—lying on their sides in the mud. Suddenly, clear as day, they could hear the steady tick, tick, tick of a watch. They looked around, trying to see where the sound was coming from, puzzled because old Ted's watch had been buried on the other side of the mine. Amos started crawling out, carrying his load, and Josh followed right behind him. But suddenly the seam caved in. Killed Josh instantly. Amos was real shook up."

Jeff and Jim finished their lunch in silence and went back to work.

"Did anyone ever find the watch?" Jim asked after a few minutes.

"Nope. But people kept hearing it. The ticking sound would move through the mine, turning up first one place, then another. Wherever it was heard, there would be a fatal accident. Luke was killed in an explosion the morning after the fire boss heard a watch ticking while he was making his nightly inspection round. Robert choked to death on some bad air the day after hearing a watch ticking in his section of the mine. And there have been others."

Jim watched Jeff carefully, trying to see if his brother-in-law was pulling his leg. But Jeff was serious. Jeff was trying to warn him.

"I've never heard it myself. And I'm right glad of it," Jeff said.

Jeff wouldn't talk about the death watch after that first day, but other miners told Jim more about it. Its tick was louder than a normal watch, and no one could predict where or when the ticking sound would turn up. The miners feared the death watch more than they feared the devil. Some miners, upon hearing the ticking sound, had tried to smash the walls with their picks in an attempt to destroy the watch. One fellow tried to blow it up with a stick of dynamite. He blew himself up instead. The death watch was relentless: ticking away the seconds of some poor man's life, ignoring the curses the miners heaped upon it, inflicting itself upon all who were marked for death.

Jim was still half-convinced that the men were playing a joke on him. According to the fire boss, the death watch had not been heard ticking for many months. Jim had just about decided to laugh off the story when young Billy Wright came running up to the seam where he was working with two other miners. Billy was shaking. "I heard the death watch. Over in Caleb's shaft. Hurry!"

They dropped everything and followed Billy at a run. They were met by a terrible wave of heat and the roar of flames.

"Fire!" Billy shouted. They raced back toward the entrance of the mine, sounding the alarm. Rescue workers poured water into the mine using water hoses until the fire was contained. Caleb was the only miner killed in the fire, which had been caused by a cable line knocked down near a wooden timber.

After the fire, Jim Kelly no longer doubted the truth of the death-watch tick. But the watch went silent, and there followed several months of peace. Jim worked so hard and so diligently that the fire boss assigned him a very tricky shaft over in a far section of the mine, a compliment to Jim's skill. Then, one morning as Jim came up the gangway, the fire boss waved him aside when Jim came up for his brass check.

"Jim," said the boss, looking very grave. "I want you to go back home."

"Go back home?" Jim asked, puzzled. Had he done something wrong? "Why? What's the matter?"

"In the name of God, Jim, go back home," the fire boss repeated. "Just do as I tell you. You'll be thanking me for it later."

Jim was frightened. He couldn't afford to be fired. He and Margaret had finally saved up enough money to rent a small cottage, but money was still very tight. Jim couldn't afford to lose a day's wages. Not with seven children to feed.

"Listen, boss. I don't understand. I thought I was giving satisfaction. Why are you calling me off?" Jim asked, feeling angry now.

The fire boss's shoulders sagged as if under a heavy weight.

"If you must know," he said slowly. "I heard the death watch ticking in your section while I was making my inspection rounds last night. If you go in there today, you won't come out."

"The death watch?" Jim gasped. He felt his heart clench, and the dinner pail rattled in his hand. Slowly, he nodded to the fire boss and turned back for home.

As he hurried toward the new cottage, Jim was filled with gratitude: He had been spared the fate of so many of his fellow miners. Glancing at his watch, he realized that he could still make the eight o'clock mass if he hurried. Wanting to give thanks for his escape from death, Jim changed quickly into his Sunday clothes and raced toward the church. When he reached the railroad grade crossing, he found the gates down. Not wishing to miss the mass, Jim jumped the gates and stepped onto the tracks.

The last thing he heard was the scream of a train whistle, as the 7:55 flyer came roaring down the tracks.

6

The Black Dog

BEDFORD COUNTY, VA

In the end, he didn't come back. All the rumors, all the malicious gossip, all the sad looks boiled down to one cruel fact: My husband—gone to scout out a new home for us in America—never came back for me. Month after hard month passed with nary a letter, not even a brief note or message sent along with a sea captain. No word. A year passed, then two. And then Civil War came to the Americas, and I lost all hope of hearing from my husband.

I bore it with a brave face as my friends stopped talking about his imminent arrival and my enemies gossiped about another woman or foreign riches, or both. As for my family, they were indignant on my behalf and didn't know what to say. Neither did I. At first I was bewildered and upset. Why hadn't I heard from him? What was causing his long delay? Then I was angry, almost believing the spiteful gossip about another woman. But as the slow years passed, so did my anger. Remembering the love we'd shared, I knew in my heart that James would never leave me for another woman. Something must have happened to him. That was the only explanation.

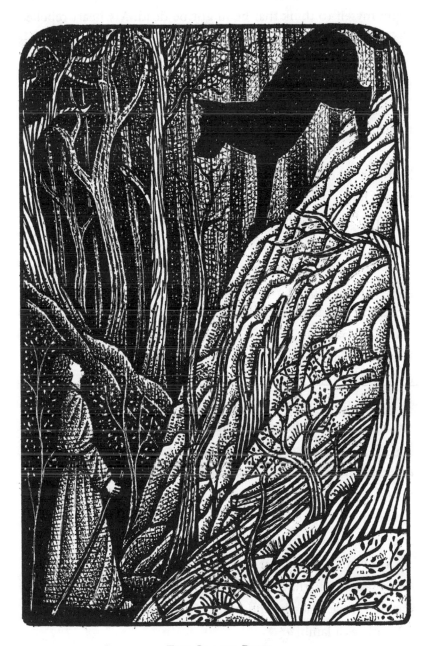

THE BLACK DOG

With this certainty came fear. Was he ill? Dying? I couldn't bring myself to think that he might be dead. My heart rebelled against it. If he was, somehow he'd let me know. My James would never leave me in suspense. He'd cross the divide somehow to speak to me.

My family and friends thought I was being extremely foolish when, on the eighth anniversary of James's departure, I announced that I was traveling to America to look for my husband. The Civil War was ended at last, and I was determined to find him.

"You'll only be hurt again," my mother said.

But I had to know what had happened to him. Even if it turned out he'd left me for another, I had to know. So I booked passage on a ship to Virginia and spent the next several seasick weeks on the high seas. I came ashore at last with only one trunk, a pocket full of money, and an empty head. Somehow I had to find James. Dead or alive, with another woman or waiting faithfully for me, I had to find him.

I was met on the dock by family friends who lived in the area. They welcomed me with open arms and offered me the first comfort I'd had in eight long years. James had stayed with them when he first arrived on his scouting trip to America, and they did not believe for a minute that he had left me. Like me, they were convinced something had happened to him and had done what they could to help me with my search.

We reminisced about old times over dinner, and my friend Alicia said, "The thing I remember best about James's last visit was that huge black hound of his. It was as large as a pony and as gentle as a lamb!"

"Lord, yes!" her husband laughed. "The beast came right into the dining room one night when we were eating roast and begged so solemnly for a taste of beef that we ended up feeding him right from the table. He sat up on his hind legs as if he were a tiny lapdog, and I swear his head was higher than mine was!"

"That sounds just like Solomon," I said with a smile. I missed our dog almost as much as I missed James. "Whenever Solomon wanted something, he reared up on his hind legs, put his paws on James's shoulders, and gazed soulfully into his eyes. Solomon was so big that he could look James right in the eyes— and James was six feet tall!"

I laughed. "He tried it with me once and knocked me right over. He was so upset that he flopped down on the floor beside me and groveled like a puppy! After that, he'd lay his head in my lap and moan when he wanted something from me!"

It felt good to laugh after all the years of pain and worry. Then my friends told me the areas where James had intended to scout for land, and together we planned my journey across Virginia.

It was a long, hard task I'd assigned myself. I stopped at one town after another, inquiring after James and his big black dog. Even after eight years, folks remembered them well. James was a gregarious soul who made a positive impression on everyone he met, and nobody could forget Solomon! Much heartened by the news, I followed in James's footsteps, viewing properties he'd prospected, talking to their owners, and staying at the same inns.

At first there was plenty of news about my missing husband. But as I got farther inland, the clues petered out. After six months of searching, I found myself grasping the smallest rumors as if they were precious pearls and trying to keep my heart from despair. Would I never learn the truth about James?

By pure chance, I happened upon a backwoods Virginian who remembered meeting James and Solomon a few years back. It was the first lead I'd had in weeks, and my heart raced with joy as he accurately described my husband and his big black dog. They had last been heard of in Bedford County, where they planned to look at a small plantation for sale. He gave me the approximate location of the plantation and the name of a good inn nearby. My heart raced as I bade him farewell. I felt as if I were getting close to my goal at last.

I also sensed something else that I wasn't yet ready to admit. Everything I had heard during my search reinforced my belief that James hadn't left me for another woman. He'd spoken so fondly of me and our life together wherever he went that I was convinced that infidelity was not behind his disappearance. But that left only one other option: Something had happened to him . . .

As soon as I set foot in the inn in Bedford County, I knew my journey was almost at an end. I could picture James and Solomon here. Their presence was so tangible that I nearly called out to them as I followed the innkeeper's wife up to my room.

After freshening up a bit, I went down to the main dining area for supper. I listened with one ear to the local residents as they sat at the bar and discussed events. I had just started eating a piece of delicious apple pie when they started talking about the black dog that haunted the pass. My head jerked up and my hand started to shake so hard that I had to put down my fork. A black dog? Solomon was a black dog.

Apparently, the black dog appeared every night at the same spot near the top of the pass. It walked back and forth along the trail as if it were guarding something. Folks traveling across the pass swore the beast was a ghost. Some claimed to have watched it pacing all night long, only to vanish with the sun's first light. According to the locals at the bar, a group of young rowdies once went to the haunted pass to see the black dog. Their horses panicked every time they drew near the huge hound, and they were forced to spend the night on the trail, unable to leave until the dog vanished with the daylight. The next night they came back to the pass, determined to kill the black dog. But their bullets passed right through his spectral body and kicked up dust on the other side. Frightened, they bolted down the trail, never to return, while behind them the black dog kept pacing back and forth, back and forth.

By this time I had covered my face with my hands, nearly bent double with pain. It couldn't be. Oh, it couldn't be! The innkeeper's wife saw my distress and hushed the patrons at the bar as she came to my side. Thinking they were frightening me, she put her plump arm around me comfortingly as she tried to lead me away upstairs. But I stopped her. Staring up into her motherly eyes, I whispered: "I must see the dog. Please, take me to the dog."

I saw a sudden flicker of understanding in her eyes. She'd been working here when James had passed through years ago. But until that moment, she'd never connected the spectral black dog with the disappearance of my husband.

Her voice husky with suppressed emotion, she called her husband, grown-up son, and a few of the more reliable patrons and asked them to ride up to the pass with me at sunset the next evening to show me the black dog. When they heard my story, they agreed.

Before we left the next evening, she made sure I was wrapped up warm and gave me a flask of whisky—"just in case." She didn't specify in case of what, but we both knew.

The ride up the pass seemed to take forever, and yet it passed too quickly. The truth was at the top of the ridge. I knew it in my bones. We rounded a bend, and in the light of the rising moon, I saw Solomon solemnly pacing along the trail ahead of us. I closed my eyes for a long, sorrowful moment. Then I slid off my horse and called my dog.

Solomon stopped abruptly and turned his great black head toward me. Then he let out a single bark of greeting and ran down the path toward me. My legs gave out and I sat down abruptly on the dirt of the path as Solomon loped up to me. When he reached me, he laid his head on my lap and moaned, just like he used to back home in England when he wanted something. I embraced him, though my arms met spectral cold where once was warm flesh.

"Where's James, Solomon?" I whispered. "Take me to James."

At once, my huge hound rose and started up the path, pausing a few feet away to make sure I was following. Behind me stalked a cadre of frightened but protective Virginia men, wanting to make sure I was safe. Solomon stopped suddenly beside a large rock at the edge of the trail. He pawed it anxiously and gave a long wail of grief. Then he vanished.

With tears streaming down my cheeks, I asked the innkeeper and his son to dig at the spot indicated by the ghost of my faithful dog. After borrowing picks and shovels from a local resident, it did not take them long to uncover the remains of a huge hound and, buried beneath it, the bones of my husband—his signet ring still on his finger. There was no sign of his purse, and we assumed he must have been robbed and slain up there on the lonely pass not long after leaving Bedford County. The robbers had killed Solomon too. Our dog was very protective and would have tried to rip out the throat of anyone attacking my husband.

We took them both back to the inn, and the local minister held a lovely funeral for my husband and his dog. I wept as he spoke of the faithfulness of Solomon, who had kept his vigil even after death, until at last he could reunite his two beloved humans.

And then, at long last, it was over. I had found the truth, and as the Good Book said, it had set me free. I could move on with my life now, and I realized in that moment that my life was not here. I did not belong in Virginia. My family was in England, and that was where I would return.

So I booked passage home, spending my last night in America with Alicia and her husband. I told my faithful friends the whole story and showed them James's signet ring, which I wore around my neck.

"Does Solomon still haunt the pass?" Alicia asked as we parted for the night.

I shook my head. "The innkeeper's son went up to the pass at sunset to watch for him one night before the funeral, but he never appeared."

"His job was done," said Alicia's husband. "Now he can rest in peace."

Yes. Now he can rest.

And may you rest in peace, my Solomon, I thought as I readied myself for bed. And thank you for watching over my James so faithfully.

7

Raw Head

Way back in the deep woods there lived a scrawny old woman who had a reputation for being the best conjuring woman in the mountains. With her bedraggled black-and-gray hair, funny eyes—one yellow and one green—and her crooked nose, Old Betty was not a pretty picture, but she was the best there was at fixing what ailed a man—and that was all that mattered.

Old Betty's house was full of herbs and roots and bottles filled with conjuring medicine. The walls were lined with strange books brimming with magical spells. Old Betty was the only one living in the Hollow who knew how to read; her granny, who was also a conjurer, had taught her the skill as part of her magical training.

Folks coming to Old Betty for a cure to their ailment sometimes peeked through the window beside her rickety porch, curious to see what was inside a conjure-woman's house. Old Betty never invited anyone in, and no one would have gone inside if she had.

Just about the only friend Old Betty had was a tough, mean, ugly old razorback hog that ran wild around her place. It rooted so much in her kitchen garbage that all the leftover

45

RAW HEAD

spells started affecting it. Some folks swore up and down that the old razorback hog sometimes walked upright like a man. One fellow claimed he'd seen the pig sitting in the rocker on Old Betty's porch, chattering away to her while she stewed up some potions in the kitchen, but everyone discounted that story on account of the fellow who told it was a little too fond of moonshine.

"Raw Head" was the name Old Betty gave the razorback, referring maybe to the way the ugly creature looked a bit like some of the dead pigs you could see come butchering time down in Hog-Scald Hollow. The razorback didn't mind the funny name. Raw Head kept following Old Betty around her little cabin and rooting up the kitchen leftovers. He'd even walk to town with her when she went to the local mercantile to sell her home remedies.

Well, folks got so used to seeing Raw Head and Old Betty in the town that it looked mighty strange one day around hog-driving time when Old Betty came to the mercantile without him.

"Where's Raw Head?" the owner asked as he accepted her basket full of home-remedy potions.

The liquid in the bottles swished in an agitated manner as Old Betty said, "I ain't seen him around today and I'm mighty worried. You seen him here in town?"

"Nobody's seen him around today. They would've told me if they did," the mercantile owner said. "We'll keep a lookout fer you."

"That's mighty kind of you. If you see him, tell him to come home straightaway," Old Betty said. The mercantile owner nodded in agreement as he handed over her weekly pay.

Old Betty fussed to herself all the way home. It wasn't like Raw Head to disappear on the day they went to town. The man at the mercantile always saved the best scraps for the mean old razorback, and Raw Head never missed a visit. When the old conjuring woman got home, she mixed up a potion and poured it onto a flat plate.

"Where's that old hog gone to?" she asked the liquid. It clouded over and then a series of pictures formed. First, Old Betty saw the good-for-nothing hunter that lived on the next ridge sneaking around the forest, rounding up razorback hogs that didn't belong to him. One of the hogs was Raw Head. She saw him taking the hogs down to Hog-Scald Hollow, where folks from the next town were slaughtering their razorbacks. Then she saw her own hog, Raw Head, slaughtered with the rest of the pigs and hung up for gutting! The final picture in the liquid was the pile of bloody bones that had once been her hog, and his scraped-clean head lying with the other hogs' heads in a pile.

Old Betty was infuriated. It was murder to her, plain and simple. Everyone in three counties knew that Raw Head was her friend, and that lazy, hog-stealing, good-for-nothing hunter on the ridge was going to pay for slaughtering him.

Now Old Betty tried to practice white magic most of the time, but she knew the dark secrets, too. She pulled out an old, secret book her granny had given her and turned to the very last page. She lit several candles and put them around the plate containing the liquid picture of Raw Head and his bloody bones. Then she began to chant: "Raw Head and Bloody Bones. Raw Head and Bloody Bones."

The light from the windows disappeared as if the sun had been snuffed out like a candle. Dark clouds billowed into the clearing where Old Betty's cabin stood, and the howl of dark spirits could be heard in the wind that pummeled the treetops.

"Raw Head and Bloody Bones. Raw Head and Bloody Bones."

Betty continued the chant until a bolt of silver lightning left the plate and streaked out through the window, heading in the direction of Hog-Scald Hollow.

When the silver light struck Raw Head's severed head, which was piled on the hunter's wagon with the other hog heads, it tumbled to the ground and rolled until it was touching the bloody bones that had once inhabited its body. As the hunter's wagon rumbled away toward the ridge where he lived, the ghost of Raw Head called out: "Bloody bones, get up and dance!"

Immediately, the bloody bones reassembled themselves into the skeleton of a razorback hog walking upright, as Raw Head had often done when he was alone with Old Betty. The head hopped on top of his skeleton, and Raw Head went searching through the woods for weapons to use against the hunter. He borrowed the sharp teeth of a dying panther, the claws of a long-dead bear, and the tail from a rotting raccoon and put them over his skinned head and bloody bones.

Then Raw Head headed up the track toward the ridge, looking for the hunter who had slaughtered him. Raw Head slipped past the thief on the road and slid into the barn where the hunter kept his horse and wagon. He climbed up into the loft and waited for the hunter to arrive.

It was dusk when the hunter drove into the barn and unhitched his horse. The horse snorted in fear, sensing the presence of Raw Head in the loft. Wondering what was disturbing his usually calm horse, the hunter looked around and saw a large pair of eyes staring down at him from the darkness above.

The hunter frowned, thinking it was one of the local kids fooling around in his barn.

"Land o' Goshen, what have you got those big eyes fer?" he snapped, thinking the kids were trying to scare him with some crazy mask.

"To see your grave," Raw Head mumbled very softly. The hunter snorted irritably and put his horse into the stall.

"Very funny. Ha, ha," The hunter said. When he came out of the stall, he saw Raw Head had crept forward a bit farther. Now his luminous yellow eyes and his bear claws could clearly be seen.

"Land o' Goshen, what have you got those big claws fer?" he snapped. "You look ridiculous."

"To dig your grave," Raw Head intoned softly, his voice a deep rumble that raised the hairs on the back of the hunter's neck. He stirred uneasily, not sure how the crazy kid in his loft could have made such a scary sound—if it really was a crazy kid.

Feeling a little spooked, he hurried to the door and let himself out of the barn. Raw Head slipped off the loft and climbed down the side of the barn behind him. With nary a rustle, Raw Head raced through the trees and up the path to a large, moonlit rock. He hid in the shadow of the stone so that the only things showing were his gleaming yellow eyes, his bear claws, and his raccoon tail.

When the hunter came level with the rock on the side of the path, he gave a startled yelp. Staring at Raw Head, he gasped: "You nearly knocked the heart right out of me, you crazy kid! Land o' Goshen, what have you got that crazy tail fer?"

"To sweep your grave," Raw Head boomed, his enchanted voice echoing through the woods, getting louder and louder with each echo.

At this point, the hunter took to his heels and ran for his cabin. He raced past the old well-house, past the wood pile, over the rotting fence, and into his yard. But Raw Head was faster. When the hunter reached his porch, Raw Head leapt from the shadows and loomed above him. The hunter stared in terror up at Raw Head's gleaming yellow eyes, his bloody bone skeleton with its long bear claws, sweeping raccoon's tail, and his razor-sharp panther teeth.

"Land o' Goshen, what have you got those big teeth fer?" he gasped desperately, stumbling backward from the terrible figure before him.

"To eat you up, like you wanted to eat me!" Raw Head roared, descending upon the good-for-nothing hunter. The thief gave one long scream in the moonlight. Then there was nothing but silence, broken by the sound of crunching.

Nothing more was ever seen or heard of the lazy hunter who lived on the ridge. His horse also disappeared that night. But sometimes folks would see Raw Head roaming through the forest in the company of his friend Old Betty. And once a month, on the night of the full moon, Raw Head would ride the hunter's horse through town, wearing the old man's blue overalls over his bloody bones with a hole cut out for his raccoon tail. In his bloody, bear-clawed hands, he carried his raw, razorback hog's head, lifting it high against the full moon for everyone to see.

8

Busted!

ASHEVILLE, NC

It was the opportunity of a lifetime. That's what Abel said. Of course, that's what Abel always said when we started a new scam. But this time, it looked like he was right. Ghost busting was the way to go, Abel said. So that was the way we went.

We needed props to make us look convincing to potential customers, so we purchased secondhand robes of a standard variety to make us look ministerial. Jacob brought along his humongous old family Bible—the kind that took two hands to lift. And I supplied several handbells thoughtfully swiped from a set when the local church lost funding from the diocese and had to shut its doors. Armed with these, a gross of white candles, and other sacred objects of the "trade," we started our new career in ghost busting.

We'd lurk in the local bars downtown and spot older citizens of a more superstitious variety. Blatant eavesdropping on the tipsy produced a few leads, and a week after our initial investment in tools, we were at the house of a little old lady called Wanda, graciously accepting tea and biscuits and hearing all about the "banging in the attic" caused by her ghost. It kept her up at night. She was always nervous. Sometimes she

BUSTED!

heard footsteps overhead. This was, Abel assured Wanda, typical ghostly behavior, and it was a good thing she'd called us to come lay the spirit to rest.

In my opinion, the show we put on was worth every penny of the exorbitant fee we charged old lady Wanda out of her retirement fund. All three of us put on robes with miters, and Abel had given me a fancy crosier he had picked up at a costume store. We staked out the attic, making a huge circle of white candles, dripping "holy water" in every corner, on every window, and all over the door. Jacob stood in the center of the candle ring holding the huge Bible and looking suitably pious. I stood beside him holding one large handbell that struck a doleful note that reverberated through the boards of the dusty attic.

Since I was the only one who had studied Latin, it was my job to do the chanting. Abel "translated" the proceedings to Wanda as we proceeded with the ceremony. My favorite moment was when Jacob's face creased with horror and he staggered backward, holding up the Bible defensively toward the "phantom of the attic." I struck a valiant pose, rang the bell rapidly several times, and threw holy water over the "ghost."

"Hallelujah! Thank you, God!" Abel shouted from his observer's position. He pumped Wanda's hand enthusiastically. "Your ghost is gone, ma'am," he told her as we sagged dramatically with relief before straightening our shoulders and cleaning up the candle ring. Wanda told us we were fine boys and wrote us a large check from her pension. Better yet, she said she'd recommend us to all her friends. Our first endorsement!

"Any banging you hear up here now is just that large branch outside your windowpane," Abel told her, leading her to the window to show her the tall oak planted too close to the house. "Any footsteps are squirrels. Your ghost is gone!"

Wanda was as good as her word. Calls started pouring in. Mostly older folks with creaky houses and time on their hands. Oh, and we had one gig where we removed a "weeping baby" from a house shared by six pretty girls just out of college. Abel got a date out of that gig while Jacob and I got bitten by the raccoon we found living in their garage. We had to get rabies shots too, which really made us mad.

"Next time, *you're* carrying that heavy Bible, and I'm holding the hand of the pretty girl," Jacob told Abel sharply. I stood in the background looking noncommittal and refrained from mentioning the visit I'd paid the girls the next day to show them the wounds the "ghost" had given me. After that visit, my dating calendar was booked solid through February!

By this time, we had more than a hundred thousand dollars in the bank, and we were sitting pretty. Everyone was happy with our "services," and the cops hadn't heard a word about us—a state of affairs that was unusual for us at this stage of the game.

Our next gig was more than an hour outside the city, deep in the Smokies. It was an old Victorian monstrosity that must have been inspired by Asheville's Biltmore House, because it was constructed on a similar—if ever so slightly smaller—scale. We turned into a ragged, overgrown driveway at dusk, and our headlights picked out the looming atrocity with its saggy old porch, cracked windowpanes, peeling paint, and rotting roof.

"Are you sure we've got the right address?" Jacob asked nervously as I navigated the car over the ruts in the gravel driveway.

"This is the place," Abel said confidently from the backseat, where he sat by the huge Bible and box of candles. "They are going to pay us fifty thousand smackeroos to get rid of their ghost! That's half again what we've already earned so far from this gig. Makes you wish you'd really gone into the priesthood."

"Or not," I said sarcastically, thinking of my pleasantly full date book.

"See, here comes our host for the evening," Abel said, pointing to a hunched figure coming down the warped front steps.

"His name isn't Igor, is it?" asked Jacob, his eyes popping. I understood exactly what he meant. The hunched white-haired fellow looked as if he was the assistant of mad Dr. Jekyll or perhaps Dr. Frankenstein himself.

"We didn't prepare for vampires," I joked nervously as the old man walked up to the door of the car.

"Will you two shut up!" Abel growled from the backseat. He threw on his "best customer" smile and leapt out of the car to greet the old man. Now that the man was visible in the headlights, I saw that the "hunch" was made by a shotgun cradled on his right arm. The man had a long, flowing beard, a gnarled old face, and the meanest black eyes you've ever seen. Oh boy! This was a real mountain man! Forget about monsters. This old fellow looked hard enough to chase us all the way to China if we didn't deliver good service tonight.

"We've got a real mean ghost tonight, boys," Abel said as we decamped from the car and began gathering our paraphernalia from the backseat. "Mr. Hatfield here says it's a screaming head. Isn't that right, Amos?"

"S'right," said the tough little man, glaring at us and fingering his shotgun thoughtfully. "'Pears on top of the main staircase and comes rolling down in flames, screaming all the way."

"Sounds ghastly," Abel said cheerfully. "But we'll soon put it to rights. Come on, fellows, let's set up in the hallway."

The inside of the house was just as warped and creepy as the outside. Cobwebs festooned the walls and ceiling. The rooms were chilly and smelled of dust and mildew. Old sheets—once white but now gray with dust—covered all the furniture, making everything look ghostly. I swear there was even one portrait on the wall of the hallway that had eyes that moved!

"Can't rent out the place," the old man said defensively when he saw my disapproving stare at all the dust piled everywhere. "Folks are too plumb scared of the haint. N'point in keeping it clean if I can't rent it. You boys set it right fer me, and I'll keep you in business 'til it's time to retire!"

Out of the corner of my eye, I saw Abel rub his hands together in glee at the notion. Personally, I wasn't so sure. Of course, I didn't believe in ghosts myself. But if any place was haunted, this would be the place!

The staircase dominated the front foyer. It was wide enough to belong in Biltmore House and ran upward for twenty-five steps before disappearing into the upper story. It had a lovely oak railing, and the wall beside it featured portraits of stern-faced ancestral types. Near the bottom was a small landing, with two stairs angling off to the right to complete the bottom of an "L." A dreadful flowered runner in a faded red went up the center of the stairs, pooled on the landing, and then continued upward past the old folks in the portraits. Someone needed to do some serious redecorating of this house once we got it "busted."

We set up our candle circle just in front of the wooden archway that framed the staircase. I lit about fifty candles while Jacob sloshed "holy" water up and down the staircase and in the corners of the room, soaking his ceremonial black robes. Somehow, Abel wriggled out of carrying the heavy Bible— again—and stood by the front door with old man Amos as I straightened the miter on my head. I nodded once to Jacob, staggering already under the weight of the massive tome, stepped into the candle circle with my crosier and handbell, and began a long chant in completely nonsensical Latin. I'd had a lot of practice lately and sounded magnificent as I droned my way up and down the scale, punctuating the sentences with mournful tolls of the bell.

I was about three-quarters of the way through my chant and was preparing to gesture with my crosier toward the "phantom" of the house, when the laughter began. It was a supernatural sound that reached inside my body and triggered every nerve ending. It had a strange echo as if the voice were laughing inside a dark cavern. I exchanged alarmed glances with Jacob as the laugh grew louder, and I sneaked a look over my shoulder at Abel, who was several shades paler than he'd been a moment before.

Then, in a tone of doom, the voice spoke.

"I come!" it cried. "I come!"

"I go! I go!" Jacob gasped beside me, nearly on his knees under the weight of the heavy Bible.

"Don't talk nonsense, man. And stand up straight!" I snapped over the heavy beating of my heart. My skin felt clammy and cold, and sweat was trickling down my forehead and across my neck.

A green light sprang up at the top of the staircase. It hovered there for a moment and then started to spin itself into a face. It was a monster face—like a Gorgon. Wild hair streamed everywhere, and sharp teeth jutted up from the wide lips. The nose was twisted and broken, and the eyes were glowing with red flames. It opened its mouth and started to scream—a horrible loud shriek that made every hair on my body stand on end. Then it burst into flames and rolled straight down the staircase toward us, making the turn at the end with the grace born of long experience. It headed right toward the candle ring!

I dropped the handbell and leapt backward, holding the crosier in front of me for protection. Unfortunately, my robes went right through the candle flames and caught fire. I staggered backward toward the door, slapping at the flames, unable to tear my horrified gaze from the approaching phantom. Its green head blazed with phantom red flames, and its scream made me want to wriggle right out of my crawling skin.

Jacob was face down in the center of the candle ring, the Bible held over his head when the phantom reached him. To my horror, I saw him rise up—Bible and all—as if he were carried on a massive wind. Then he was tossed right past me through one of the wide windows framing the door. Jacob gave a shout of terror as glass shattered everywhere. Abel and I were littered with the shards, and tiny red cuts covered my face and hands.

I noticed peripherally that Amos seemed to have disappeared from the hallway, but that was all I had time to note before the head came for me. Abel was struggling desperately with the latch on the front door as the phantom wind wrapped around me with the force of a giant's fist. I was sent flying upward right through the ceiling. Plaster and boards and jagged ends of wood cascaded around me. I would have been knocked out if I hadn't had the miter on my head. I was lifted so high that my head hit the ceiling of the third story before the phantom fist dropped me onto the second-story floor. Somehow, I rolled onto my feet and dove straight for the front window. Thankfully, my subconscious remembered there was a front porch. I fell only a few feet before I hit the rotting roof of the porch and crashed through it, down onto the glass-strewn boards below.

Inside the house I heard Abel screaming. The front door burst open beside me, and Abel staggered backward through it, covered in glowing green flames. The bodiless head was laughing again, and it was three times the size it had been when it first appeared. I leapt to my feet, grabbed Abel by the flaming arm—a heroic act on my part—and hustled him off the porch into the yard. Jacob was in the car already, frantically trying to turn around in the narrow driveway. We approached the car at a run. I wrenched open the door and flung Abel and myself into the back seat.

Fortunately for all, the green flames covering Abel extinguished as soon as we entered the vehicle. Jacob gunned the motor, and we raced out of the driveway and down the hill with such speed that the wheels of the car sometimes left the ground on the tighter curves. None of us spoke. We were shaking with reaction, and all of us were bleeding from the cuts we'd received when the window broke. Plus, I had a huge bump on my head where it had crashed through the ceiling.

Jacob didn't slow the car until we reached the outskirts of Asheville. "I don't know about you two, but my ghost-busting days are over," he announced as we entered the city. Abel and I heartily concurred.

I found out later that Abel had gotten tipsy when he went out with the pretty girl from the crying-baby house and had let it slip that a raccoon—not a ghost—had inflicted those wounds on Jacob and me. Since her family ran an illegal moonshine business on the side, she didn't want to go to the police about our little scam. So, she asked her Uncle Amos to introduce us to a real ghost to pay us back for our little deception. In the end, we were the ones who got busted!

9

One Fine Funeral

KNOXVILLE, TN

I've been living next door to the Henslee family for nigh on forever, and it saddened me when they died off over the years, until only Addie Bell and her brother Cass were left at the old homestead.

Addie Bell could have married any number of fellows who courted her over the years, but instead, she devoted herself to her younger brother Cass, who hadn't as much gumption as Addie Bell and just scraped by doing the minimum to keep body and soul together. It was Addie Bell who did the cooking and the cleaning and the sewing. She kept a farm garden, so they had plenty to eat and she managed all the money for the household, including paying the insurance premiums so they'd have money for their burying when the time came for them to depart this troubled world. As for Cass, well, he'd take a part-time job here and there, never for long. When it got hard, he quit. He was happy to let Addie Bell support the family.

This state of affairs went on for many years, until Addie Bell was well past the marrying stage and Cass was a fine-looking man in his forties. Then one day, Cass came over to sit with me on the front porch and deliver some surprising news. He'd

One Fine Funeral

been walking out with a girl called Josephine Foxhall for about a month, and no one thought much of it. Cass had been courting this girl and that one ever since he was grown, and nothing came of it. So, when Cass told me that he and Josephine had decided to get married, you could have knocked me off my porch with a feather, I was that surprised.

"Truly?" I asked.

"Truly," he replied, beaming with pride. "We are getting married tomorrow week."

I congratulated him, as was proper. Then a thought struck me. How would this impact Addie Bell, who had devoted her whole life to her younger brother? I asked cautiously: "What does Addie Bell have to say about it?"

Cass shrugged. "Dunno. I ain't told her yet." Then he grinned and jumped to his feet. "Now's as good a time as any! Wish me luck." He winked at me and loped next door to the Henslee house to speak to his sister.

"Good luck," I said faintly. I had a sinking feeling in the pit of my stomach. I didn't think Addie Bell would be pleased with this turn of events.

I went inside to pour myself a cold glass of lemonade, and by the time I got back to the front porch, the whole neighborhood could hear what Addie Bell thought about the upcoming marriage. She ranted about her brother's laziness, and his lack of sense, and how stuck-up she thought Josephine was.

"You're so lazy, you don't even pay your own funeral insurance premiums," Addie Bell shouted. "If I didn't make them quarterly payments, you'd have nowhere to be buried, you rascal. If you can't even do something that simple, how are you going to support a wife? You ain't bringing her here!"

"Josephine's got enough gumption to support the both of us," Cass retorted. "And while we're speaking of the funeral insurance, let me tell you: A man's wife is duty bound to get his insurance. Everybody knows that. I told Josephine you wouldn't mind making her the beneficiary from now on, seeing she's going to be my wife."

Addie Bell hit the roof when she heard this request. I thought she'd been loud before, but the way she started screaming and ranting sent Cass running for the door. "You told her I wouldn't mind?" she roared after him as he bolted down the front walkway. "I'll see you toasting rabbits on a pitchfork in Hell before I let that stuck-up woman collect any insurance that I paid benefits on!"

Everybody on the block was looking out their windows or watching from the porch as Cass raced down the street and skidded around the corner on his way to Josephine's place.

Cass didn't dare set foot in the old Henslee house that night. He slept on the floor at my place instead. He snuck home around noontime to test the waters, and Addie Bell sent him away in a hot minute, screaming awful things about him and his chosen lady.

Cass laid low for another couple of nights before trying again. This time, Addie Bell let him in the house, though she grumbled and complained any time he tried to mention his upcoming wedding, which was this coming Saturday at the church. Still, she was much calmer than before, so Cass broached the subject of the insurance again, seeing that the agent was stopping by to collect on the benefit the following day.

"Well, I been thinking about it, and I suppose there's something to what you say," Addie Bell said grudgingly. "I'll make over the insurance as soon as you and Josie get hitched this weekend. But you'll have to pay the company from now on. I'm done with that."

Cass was delighted. He'd promised Josephine that he'd bring Addie Bell around to their way of thinking, and he had! He gave his sister a sloppy kiss on the cheek and ran off to tell his intended bride the good news.

Cass wasn't there when the insurance man came, so he didn't know that Addie Bell doubled the insurance coverage on her brother, so it cost fifty cents a week where before it only cost twenty-five. I heard the two of them bargaining through the kitchen window, which was open to let in the breeze, and I told myself this must be Addie Bell's way of getting even with Cass for marrying Josephine. I didn't think the newlyweds would be pleased about the new price, but it wasn't my business to interfere. At least Addie Bell had come around to the marriage, which was a better situation than before.

On Friday night, Addie Bell fixed Cass a fine supper in celebration of their last night together as a family. She made all his favorite dishes; turnip greens, a whole hog jowl, poke salad, corn pone, buttermilk, fried chicken, and a big pot of black-eyes peas with hot pepper chow-chow. The smell of that meal wafted over to my porch and made my mouth water. I almost invited myself to dinner, but I figured they'd want to be alone when they said goodbye. After the wedding tomorrow, Cass would live across town at Josephine's place, and Addie Bell would stay by herself in the old Henslee homestead.

I was reading the newspaper on my porch swing when Cass waddled out his front door and sat down on the stoop, looking as happy and satisfied as any man alive after that massive meal.

He waved to me before taking out his old corn-cob pipe and having a smoke. He was too full to talk, so we happily ignored one another. Cass would be over when he was good and ready to discuss his new life with Josephine, just like he had every night since he got engaged.

All at once, Cass gave a terrible holler and clutched his belly. He bent double and rolled down to the ground, curled up in a ball of pain. As I leapt up in alarm, he shouted: "Oh help me, Addie Bell. I'm dying! Call me a doctor, quick."

Addie Bell yelled out the window: "Oh hush, Cass. You've eaten too much, that's all. You need some peppermint tea, not a doctor. I'll put the kettle on."

I wasn't so sure. Cass was real pale and writhing on the ground. I ran down my front steps and jumped the fence between our yards. The neighbors across the way came running too, alarmed by the screams and moans coming from the front stoop of the Henslee house.

"Addie Bell," I shouted as Cass made one final spasm and then lay very still. I reached him at the same time as the neighbors from across the street. We bent over him and realized at once that Cass was gone. "Addie Bell," I shouted again. She came out of the house, looking puzzled.

"What's going on?" she asked. Then she caught sight of Cass, lying so still on the ground, and she clapped a hand over her mouth, her eyes going wide.

"It's too late for the doctor," the neighbor from across the street told Addie Bell before his wife could hush him. Addie Bell's eyes rolled back in her head, and she fainted right there in the doorway.

Everyone on the block gathered round poor dead Cass, and they whispered to one another: "Poor Cass! He died hard, yes, he did. He's gone and left poor Addie and poor Josie."

One ancient fellow shook his head and said: "It looks bad for poor Addie, don't you know. When they die hard, they come back to haunt you. Just you watch."

The others hushed him and helped carry Cass into the house. They laid his body out on the bed and put coins on his eyes. Then they turned the mirror and pictures to the wall and started to moan and wail and pray over the departed.

We put smelling salts under Addie's nose 'til she woke up. I got her a cup of lemonade, but she set it aside and told me she had to call the insurance company right away. I didn't think it was right, calling the insurance before anyone had even notified the bride to be that the wedding was off, but that's the way Addie Bell did things. She got the insurance doctor to come by right away, and he asked her a few questions about how old Cass was and how he died. Then he filled out some papers to say Cass died with acute indigestion—which means a godawful bellyache—and that was that, as far as the law and the insurance company were concerned. It wasn't till after Addie Bell called the undertaker and told him to go all out with the funeral that someone finally went over to tell Josephine that the wedding was off.

Once the arrangements were made and Cass was laying out on the cooling board, Addie Bell called some mourners to come in and set up with her, and that's when she finally started to moan and carry on. It was mighty peculiar. It felt like Addie Bell had done everything backward.

What exactly was going on at the Henslee house, I wondered. How come Cass had died on this particular Friday; the day *before* his wedding and two days *after* Addie Bell bumped up his insurance premium? No matter which way I looked at it, things didn't seem right. But what could I do? The doctor had signed papers saying Cass died of indigestion, so that was that, as far as the law was concerned.

When Josephine looked in, Addie Bell treated her like a long-lost sister, and they cried on each other's necks. It kind of turned my stomach, after hearing the way Addie Bell raged about the girl just a few days before. I made up an excuse and went home, real disturbed in my thinking.

Folks sat up with the dead for three nights and two days, as was the custom in those days, moaning and mourning with the last of the Henslee family. Then everyone came from far and wide to attend Cass's funeral. The church house was packed full, until the walls almost bulged out. Old, young, rich, poor, near and far, everyone came to the church to send Cass Henslee off in style.

Addie Bell had gone all out for the funeral, what with all the extra money she'd gotten from the updated insurance policy. There was a fancy awning stretched over the six-by-six hole at the grave site so folks attending the ceremony would stay dry in case of rain. There was a striped canopy running from the church door all the way out to the street. They'd decorated the old church from floor to rooftop with ferns and flowers and black ribbons. Addie Bell was wearing a fancy new black dress, and she had ordered the finest of fine coffins for her brother. It had gold handles and a silk lining. Cass was wearing a fancy suit that he wouldn't have ever picked out for himself, and he looked kind of peaceful lying there. Everyone in the church said this was one fine funeral Addie Bell had put together for her little brother.

I felt mighty uncomfortable looking at all those decorations bought with the insurance money. I reckoned Cass would rather be wedding with Josephine than laid out in funeral splendor, but he didn't get a vote in the matter. Since the insurance doctor had signed his death certificate saying he died of indigestion, no one was going to drag Addie Bell to the courthouse and accuse her of murder. This wasn't right, but there wasn't anything I could do about it except pray the Lord would take care of it, somehow.

Well, the preacher took to preaching with such vigor that we were there for a full three hours hearing about how kind Cass had been and how beautiful heaven was and how he'd be waiting there for his poor Josephine and his generous sister Addie Bell and how all the angels would be singing there before the good Lord. When the preacher finally wound down his sermon, he beckoned to Addie Bell to come up front among the heaped-up piles of flowers and ferns. She stood right beside Cass in his coffin and led the whole congregation in the last hymn, which was "Steal Away."

Addie Bell belted out the words in her fine mezzo soprano. She gripped the side of the coffin with one hand and swayed back and forth like a sapling in a windstorm. And the congregation, they were singing and stomping with her, slow and solemn. By the second verse, the whole church was a-creaking and a-groaning until it sounded like it was mourning with us. And suddenly, the whole front of the church gave way. The rafters cracked and busted loose. The walls sagged inward, raining shingles on everyone in the front pews. The organ pitched forward, missing the pulpit and the coffin by a whisker and falling right smack dab on Addie Bell. For a tense second, everything was still, and I thought it might be over. Then the whole floor gave way. Organ, pulpit, coffin and all plummeted eight feet down to the dirt floor below, and the rafters caved in above them.

When the coffin hit the floor of the cellar, Cass's body flew out. He landed against one of the posts that supported the floor, and there he sat with his dead eyes staring accusingly at Addie Bell and one arm flung straight out to point at the place where her body lay, squashed flat by the heavy organ. Nobody else was hurt.

After that, there was no question in anyone's mind that Addie Bell had poisoned her brother Cass to keep him from marrying Josephine Foxhall. And the Lord God Almighty struck her dead for her meanness.

It was one fine funeral, sure enough. Folks in the neighborhood still talk about it to this day.

10

The Bell Witch

ADAMS, TN

"I warn you, Sally-girl," Granny said to me one hot summer afternoon as we sat on the front porch drinking ice-cold glasses of homemade lemonade, "there are probably a hundred different versions of the Bell Witch story floating around the country. All I can tell you about the Bell Witch is the story as it was told to me by my great granddaddy. If you want 'truth' and 'facts,' you would do better to read one of the books that have been written about the Bell Witch."

"I would like to hear your story," I said promptly, bouncing a bit in my chair from pure excitement. Granny gave me a look that told me she did not consider my behavior up to the standards of a Southern lady. I sat still.

"The Bell family," Granny began, "moved to Robertson County sometime around 1804. They were a God-fearing family who were leading members of the community. The spirit that plagued the Bell family first made its presence known in 1817. According to my great granddaddy, the spirit commenced its activities by rapping on the walls of the house. Shortly thereafter, it began pulling the quilts off the children's beds, tugging on their hair, and slapping and pinching them until red

72

THE BELL WITCH

marks appeared on their faces and bodies. It would steal sugar right out of the bowl, spill the milk, and taunt the Bell family by laughing and cursing at them. Really, it was quite a rude spirit!" Granny paused to give her opinion. She took a dainty sip of lemonade and continued her story.

"Naturally, all this hullabaloo caused great excitement throughout the community. People would come from miles around to meet this spirit, which would gossip with them and curse at them and play tricks on them. According to my great-granddaddy, John Bell and his family would feed and entertain all these guests at their own expense—not an easy task. The house would get so full that people were forced to camp outside.

"When Old Hickory heard about the Bell Witch, he decided to pay a visit to the Bell home. The general brought a party up with him from Nashville. They filled a wagon with provisions and tents for camping out, to avoid discomforting the Bell family.

"General Jackson and his party approached the plantation, laughing and talking about the witch and all its pranks. The men were on horseback, following the wagon with their supplies. They were boasting of how they would best the Bell Witch, when suddenly the wagon stopped short. Tug and pull as they might, the horses could not move the wagon an inch, even though they were on flat ground with no trace of mud. The driver shouted and snapped the whip, but the horses could not shift the wagon. General Jackson asked all the horsemen to dismount, and together they pushed against the wagon, to no avail. The wagon would not budge.

"Old Hickory had the men examine the wheels one by one—taking them off, checking the axles, and then reattaching them. There was nothing wrong with the wheels. They tried to move the wagon again, whipping up the horses, shouting, and pushing. But still the wagon would not budge. The men were completely flummoxed. What was going on? Then the general shouted, 'Boys, it's the witch!'

"An eerie voice answered Old Hickory from the shrubbery: 'All right, General. Let the wagon move on. I will see you again tonight.'

"The men looked around in astonishment, for they had seen no one nearby. At once, the horses started moving without any prompting from the coachman, and the wagon rumbled along the road as if it had never been stuck at all.

"Old Hickory and his men were sobered by their strange experience. Suddenly the idea of camping out was not very appealing, even though one of their men was supposed to be a professional witch tamer.

"When the general's party reached the house, John Bell and his wife extended every courtesy to their distinguished guest and his friends, offering them food, drink, entertainment, and quarters for the night. But Old Hickory had only one entertainment in mind. He had come for witch hunting, and nothing else would do. After dining with the Bells, the whole party sat waiting for the spirit to appear. To while away the time, they listened to the boasts of the witch tamer, who had a gun with a silver bullet that he meant for the spirit. The men were secretly amused by the man's vanity, yet they found his presence oddly comforting after their strange experiences with the wagon. Here was someone who could handle the spirit.

"The hour grew late. Old Hickory was restless, and the men were getting drowsy. The witch tamer began taunting the spirit and playing with his gun. Suddenly, there was the sound of footsteps crossing the floor. Everyone snapped to attention. Then the same eerie voice they had heard on the road exclaimed, 'I am here. Now shoot me!'

"The witch tamer aimed his gun at the place where they had heard the voice. He pulled the trigger, but the gun didn't fire. The spirit began to taunt him as the witch tamer tried to shoot the gun again. Then the spirit said, 'Now it's my turn.'

"Everyone heard the sounds of the witch tamer being slapped silly as he shouted, 'Lordy, Lordy!' and 'My nose!' and 'The devil's got me!' He began to dance about the parlor, screaming that the spirit was pricking him with pins and beating him. Then the door swung open of its own accord and the witch tamer raced outside, still shouting 'Lordy, Lordy!' as he ran down the lane. Everyone followed him outside, expecting him to drop dead, but aside from an occasional jump, twist, or shout, the witch tamer seemed likely to live. They watched him as he ran out of sight, while Old Hickory laughed until his sides were sore.

"They were all startled when they heard the spirit's voice among them again. It was laughing at its triumph over the witch tamer and claimed that there was another fraud in the group that it would expose the next night. The men were pretty shaken up when they heard the spirit's words. It was one thing to laugh at a fake witch tamer who got his comeuppance. It was quite another thing to realize one of them might be the next target. Old Hickory was all set to stay a full week with the Bells, but his men were not so enthusiastic.

"My great granddaddy didn't know exactly what happened that night to change Old Hickory's mind. Maybe the spirit played some pranks on him, maybe the justifiable fear of his men persuaded him. Whatever the case, General Andrew Jackson was up and away the next morning. By dark, Old Hickory's party had already reached Springfield and they went on to Nashville the next day. Much later, Old Hickory was heard to remark, 'I'd rather fight the entire British Army than deal with the Bell Witch.'"

Granny took a sip of her lemonade and shook her head. "I don't blame the general one bit for leaving so quickly. I would have done the same thing."

"What happened to the Bell Witch?" I asked.

"Oh, most of the stories agree that the Bell Witch got worse and worse, tormenting Betsy Bell something awful and finally poisoning John Bell so that he died. They say the spirit laughed and sang in triumph at John's funeral. The spirit stayed for several months following the death of John Bell, putting pressure on Betsy to break her engagement with a man named Gardener, which Betsy did sometime around Easter of 1821. After that, the spirit told Mrs. Bell that it was going away, but would visit again in seven years."

"Did it come back?" I asked.

"Yes, the spirit did return to visit the family seven years later, just as it promised," said Granny. "For about three weeks, the spirit talked with John Bell Jr., making predictions about the future, and promising to return in one hundred and seven years. As far as I know, the Bell family did not receive the second promised visit. I have heard some people claim that the Bell Witch never really left the Bells' property, but still haunts the land to this day. I myself have not gone there to find out if this is true."

Granny finished her lemonade and peered at me from under the rim of her straw hat. "Well, Sally-girl, that's enough about evil spirits for one day. I am going back to my garden. Get along with you now. And don't forget those tomatoes I set aside for your mama."

"Yes, ma'am," I said meekly, taking my glass back to the kitchen before I started for home.

11

Dispatched

GREENVILLE, SC

There was something odd in the tone of the dispatcher's voice when he called to tell me a person needed picking up at Bramlett Road late one summer night in 1947. I shuddered when I heard the name of the street, and I glanced inadvertently at my watch. Nearly midnight. I did not want to go anywhere near that area at midnight. But I drove a Yellow Cab, and it was my job to pick up a call when it came. I swallowed and started the car with sweaty palms, heading toward Bramlett Road and the slaughter yards.

I'd been out of town when the incident happened. I call it an incident, but it was murder, plain and not so simple. The dispatcher told me the story when I got home, and he'd looked a little green when he spoke about what happened. One of the fellows who drove a cab with our company—name of Brown— was robbed and stabbed to death in his cab. That was bad. I knew Brown slightly, and I'd liked him. His death saddened me, and it worried me too. You spend a lot of time alone in your cab, and when you're not alone, it's because you are driving strangers around town. In my experience, not all of those strangers were nice; a fact Brown could attest to, had he lived.

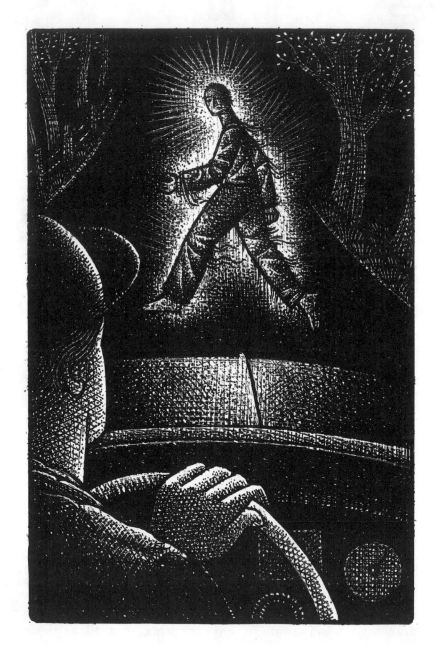

DISPATCHED

Anyhow, the dispatcher said they caught the fellow who had done it. A man named Willie Earle was picked up by the police the very next day and put in jail. 'Course, his family stoutly denied that he'd had anything to do with the murder. Said Willie had come home the previous day on the bus and hadn't used a cab at all. But there's no smoke without fire, the dispatcher said. Willie's family would say something like that, and the police around here were pretty good about finding the man who committed a crime.

I thought the story would end there, but the dispatcher kept on talking, and my heart sank as I listened to the rest of it. Apparently a bunch of hotheads who drove cabs for our company gathered together in the office, passing around a bottle of whiskey and talking about "getting" the fellow who'd stabbed Brown. One of the men went out and borrowed a shotgun, and a few minutes later a procession of cabs drove to the old jailhouse where Willie Earle was kept. Once the jailer saw the mob and the guns, he let them into the jail, and the mob grabbed Earle and threw him in the back of one of the cabs. They drove over to the slaughter yards, where they roughed him up a bit in the backseat. Then one man pulled a knife, and they dragged Earle forcibly from the back—had to pry his fingers loose from the seat. The men started hitting him with their fists and the stock of the shotgun, and the knife-wielder waded in and really made a mess. According to the dispatcher, Earle shouted: "Lord, you've killed me!" Then one of the cab drivers called for the shotgun and put a bullet in his head. They reloaded and shot him twice more. When they were sure he was dead, the mob climbed back into their separate cabs and fanned out, each heading back to Greenville by a different route.

The dispatcher started to give me the names of the men in the mob, but I made him shut up. I didn't want to know. Oh, I could probably guess without much difficulty. I'd been working in the company for years, and I knew the fellows pretty well by now. But it was better that I not know anything more than he'd told me, so I could deny any knowledge of the incident if I was questioned about it. Not that it did much good. Word got around soon enough, and thirty-one fellows were arrested for the crime. A few months later, they were all acquitted by a jury of their peers.

I was still thinking about dead Willie Earle as I drove along Bramlett Road, searching the area for my passenger, who'd told the dispatcher he'd be waiting on the side of the road near the slaughter yards. I slowed down to a crawl, glancing this way and that in the bright glow of the headlights. No one was there. Finally, I parked the cab on the side of the road and got out to have a quick smoke while I waited for my passenger to show up.

I stood in the darkness next to my car, the smoke from my cigarette helping to mask the stench from the slaughter yards. It was a cloudy night, and the wind ruffled my hair and swirled oddly in the tall grass at my feet. The only light came from the end of my cigarette as I smoked.

All at once, the temperature around me plummeted. It felt as if I were standing outside in midwinter. My breath came out as a puff of white steam in the red glow from the end of my cigarette. I froze in place, suddenly terrified, my heart thumping heavily against my ribs. Was that a groan I heard? Had my passenger been hurt?

The moan came again, and then I heard a voice crying: "I swear, it wasn't me. I don't know who did it!" A man began to scream. The sound tore through me like a razor blade, scraping my nerves raw. I dropped my cigarette and fumbled with the car door as the air around me grew colder. Now I could hear the unmistakable thud of hammering fists. The darkness of the night was filled with swirling black silhouettes pounding on something . . . or someone. I caught a glint of metal—tinged with the red glow from the dying cigarette lying on the ground—as my hands closed on the icy-cold door handle. Then I heard the sound of fabric ripping, and I heard a man scream again in agony. The scream muted into terrible words: "Lord, you've killed me!" Another voice shouted for a gun, and I heard one shot, followed swiftly by two more.

I wrenched the door open with shaking hands and threw myself inside the cab. It took me two tries to get the engine started, and then I squealed the tires as I spun the cab around. Something was standing in the middle of the road, blocking my path. It was a tall, battered figure that glowed just enough for me to see its lolling head, the blood-stained, dead features, the knife-torn clothes. It reached toward the cab with bloody hands. I screamed and swerved to avoid it. Then I floored the gas pedal and sped from the gruesome place as fast as the cab would take me.

I slammed into the office a few moments later and told the dispatcher I was quitting. Then I grabbed my things and headed home. My missus had died a few years back and my kids were all grown and flown, so there was no need to stay here. I'd get a job in Columbia or maybe down in Charleston where my daughter lived. One thing was for sure: There was no way I was staying in this haunted town.

Treasure

She was elderly, impoverished, and tired. So very tired. She had been mistress of the local day school until her eyesight gave out. But the little she had saved from her meager teacher's salary was barely enough to keep body and soul together.

When the cheap boardinghouse in which she had resided for more than thirty years was purchased by a greedy man at the end of the Civil War, the old lady knew she was in trouble. The man didn't care two pennies for any of the old-timers living in his new property. He sent a letter to all the tenants announcing that he had raised the rent, and he laughed when the old-timers gave him a piece of their collective minds.

As far as the new landlord was concerned, there were plenty of people out there who would pay high prices for their board and be glad to have a roof over their heads. And he was right. Soon the boardinghouse filled up with former soldiers and businessmen.

The old lady, who had nowhere else to go, was uncomfortable among the new tenants. She knew that the landlord was looking for an excuse to evict her. And it would not be long in coming.

TREASURE

The high rent was eating into her savings. It would not be long before her money was gone.

On the first day of January—New Years Day—the old schoolteacher counted her money and knew it was not enough to pay the rent. She went to the landlord with the partial payment, and he ordered her to vacate immediately. Mute with terror, the old lady packed her meager belongings into an ancient black valise and walked down the stairs of the boardinghouse for the last time. The landlord locked the door of her room behind her and took away her key.

The old schoolteacher stood on the creaky front porch and stared blindly at the street, wondering what to do. She had no family, and all her friends were dead. It was colder than normal this winter. She could not sleep outside.

Shivering, the old lady pulled her coat tightly around her, tucking a scarf around her wrinkled neck. She started walking aimlessly down the road, the heavy bag leaving welts on her skinny old hands. Her worn gloves quickly tore under this harsh treatment. She pulled the tattered remains from her hands and stuck them in a pocket. She stopped frequently, setting the bag down and staring into the woods around her as she shook life back into her stinging palms. Her mind was a blank. She could not think about the future. She just walked and walked and walked.

As the light began to fail, the old lady found herself walking down an overgrown lane leading toward the abandoned Fox residence. Folks in town never came here. It was said that a headless ghost haunted the house and grounds. But she was desperate for a roof over her head and didn't care if a thousand ghosts lived in the house. She could stay here until she found a new home.

The old lady picked up her heavy bag and trudged through the weedy lane as shadows deepened around her. She could see the weathered old bridge looming ahead of her in the gloom. In the light of the gibbous moon rising majestically over the oak trees, she studied the bridge. The boards were warped, and there was a huge, splintered hole in the floor through which she could see the water a long way below. The roof was covered in moss and sagged in the middle.

The old lady stopped and stared at the rickety structure, frightened to go on. What if it collapsed under her feet? She would drown in the rushing water below. But she had no choice. It was either risk the bridge or let her old body freeze in the unsheltered night air.

Straightening her shoulders, the old lady stepped cautiously onto the creaky bridge, keeping to one side to avoid the hole in the floor. Around her the temperature plummeted like a stone. Wind gusted through the tunnel, knocking her sideways into the wall as a sepulchral voice began to moan. "Ooooooohhhhhhhh!" the voice wailed on the wind. "Oooooooohhhhhhhh!"

The old lady fell to her knees in dismay. Surely this must be the voice of the ghost! Dare she go on? But she must or freeze to death in the darkness of the covered bridge. Keeping one trembling old hand on the splintered wall for balance, the old lady pushed through the forceful wind that howled through the covered bridge. At long last she stepped into the moonlit lane and stood facing the ruined Fox house.

The wind was even stronger in the lane, swirling around her like a cyclone, snatching at the scarf around her wrinkled neck.

The old lady freed one rubbed-raw hand from the black bag to clutch at her scarf, staring in dismay at the sinister old house with its ruined porch and dark windows that stared at her like the eyes of a hungry beast.

"Ooooooooohhhhhhhh," moaned the wind. "Ooooooooo-hhhhhhhh!"

She heard the sound of galloping hooves crossing the bridge behind her. The old lady whirled, cold sweat breaking out all over her wrinkled body. Her old heart was beating so hard she thought it would burst. A glowing figure burst forth from the covered bridge. The man atop the ghostly steed wore the costume of a Revolutionary soldier, and he had no head!

The old lady stood paralyzed, staring at the headless horseman galloping toward her at speed. The black bag slipped from her hands, and she raised her stinging palms in a gesture of repudiation, as if her will alone could stop the phantom's approach. Closer it came, and still closer. The old lady's legs trembled beneath her, too weak to run. Her eyes were fixed on the terrible figure, and she could feel them drying in the howling wind. Please, God, let it be over quickly, she prayed silently. The horse reared above her, hooves flailing the air.

The old lady closed her eyes in despair. And then she heard a voice inside her head.

"At last! You have come at last!"

It was a man's voice. His tone was one of relief and joy. The old lady opened her eyes in astonishment. The horse was standing now, watching her with dark eyes that glowed from within. The headless figure on its back was holding one hand toward her, palm up, beseeching her to listen, to understand.

"My lady," the headless horseman said into her mind, "in life I was a miser who cherished money above all else. I ruined many innocent people who owed me money, and more than one child was orphaned by my neglect. When I was summoned to war, I buried my treasure here on this land to keep it safe until my return. But a cannonball decapitated me during battle, and my treasure remains hidden to this day. If I had been blameless, my spirit would have gone directly to heaven. But for my crimes, my spirit was tied to this place, doomed to ride this lane forever unless some brave soul should ask me to reveal the location of my treasure. Will you ask, dear lady, and release my spirit from this place?"

The old lady took a deep breath, her ribs aching from her terrible fright.

"Please, sir, will you tell me where your treasure is buried?" she quavered, trembling with cold and fear.

Directions to the treasure poured into the old lady's mind. With the final word spoken, the phantom gave a mighty shout. The light glowing through horse and headless rider grew in intensity until the old lady was forced to shield her eyes. For a moment the world went white. Then the old lady was alone in the darkness, with her black bag and her pounding heart. And half a million dollars buried twenty feet from the place she stood.

It is amazing what a body—even an old one—can do with the proper motivation. With the help of a dilapidated shovel discovered in a ruined tool shed, the old lady dug up a trunk full of gold coins and dragged it into the house, using an impromptu travois like the ones she had made with the schoolchildren many years ago. She lit a fire in the old fireplace and sat eating a dried apple—all the food she had left—while she counted her newfound wealth.

In the morning the old lady went to the bank and deposited the money. In the afternoon she went to the lawyer of her former landlord and offered him cash on the barrelhead for the boardinghouse.

On the third day of January, the old lady evicted her evictor and moved back into her old home for good. Using her newfound gold, she renovated the old boardinghouse, turning it into a real home with proper furniture and servants and a fancy butler to open her front door to visitors.

When folks in town asked the old lady how she had come by her good fortune, she told them it was an unexpected inheritance from an old friend. Which was the exact truth. She never went into details, though, for who would believe her if she did?

13

The Bell Ringer

ATLANTA, GA

"Honestly, that boy could get away with murder!"

His mother's oft-repeated complaint rang through the thief's mind as he drove his stiletto into the bell ringer's back, piercing the man's beating heart. The bell ringer slumped into the dirt of the deserted alleyway, blood pouring from the wound. The thief smiled grimly as he searched the man's pockets for the keys to the bell tower. Getting away with murder was the easy part, he reckoned. It was retrieving the stolen money that was proving difficult. His fingers closed around the keys, lying deep inside the man's waistcoat. At last! The thief hurried out of the alleyway, leaving the bell ringer behind in a congealing pool of blood.

It was a pity it had come to this. The bell ringer was a nice sort. But he was in the way, and the thief couldn't let a mere bell ringer stand between him and the small fortune he'd left in the bell tower of the church after the bank robbery.

If only the sheriff and his men had not been hard on his tail after the theft! But the constabulary had been everywhere, and the thief was forced to stash his stolen money in the first place he could find. Which happened to be the local bell tower,

THE BELL RINGER

where ringers were practicing the Sunday carillon. The thief had hidden in the base of the tower until the last bell ringer left, then carried the currency-filled cardboard box upstairs and stashed it on a back shelf underneath a coil of rope.

The thief waited for three nights, until furor over the bank theft abated, before attempting to retrieve the stolen money. But when he visited the church, the door to the tower was locked. The thief swore several times. He didn't dare pound on the church doors and demand entry, for what explanation could he give for wanting in at midnight? He had no tools to break down the massive portal and no skill at picking locks.

Frustrated, the fuming thief hurried home. He had to get into the belfry tonight. He couldn't afford to wait for next week's bell practice. Wanted signs with his sketched likeness were posted all over town. His senses screamed at him to leave Atlanta, but the thief wasn't going anywhere without that box of money.

In the afternoon the thief visited the minister of the church, pretending interest in becoming a member. He spoke eloquently of his love for music in general and for church bells in particular. The obliging minister gave him the name of the director of the bell ringers, who would be delighted to have a new recruit.

Once he had a name, the thief tracked down the man with little difficulty and waited in a back alley while the man had drinks at an inn on the outskirts of town. When the bell ringer stepped outside for a breath of fresh air, the waiting thief attacked.

Leaving the dead bell ringer in the alleyway, the thief fled through the maze of streets toward the church. The bell tower loomed darkly against the night sky, silhouetted by the light of a waxing gibbous moon. He was almost to his destination when he saw a policeman sitting in a dilapidated old guardhouse that stood opposite the church. The thief swore and slid behind a tree to watch the man. No one had manned that guardhouse in years. Why now—tonight of all nights? The thief knew the answer. There was a bank robber loose in Atlanta. The sheriff had doubled the number of men on duty, and they grew more aggressive with each passing day.

The thief lurked in the shadows, hoping the policeman would head out on his beat. He only needed one chance to slip into the bell tower and get the box of money. Then he'd be out of town on the next train heading west. He waited for an hour, both anxious and bored. He still had his knife. After killing the bell ringer, it didn't seem such a stretch to kill the policeman as well to attain his goal. But the policeman was armed.

Out of options, the thief crept down the street toward the guardhouse and crouched beneath the back window, feeling for the sash. The policeman sat eating a sandwich and idly watching the street. Suddenly the policeman stood up and hurried to the front window. He stared at the church, feeling for his gun. The thief froze in place and then crept to the side of the building to look at the church, wondering what had caught the policeman's attention. At first glance the thief saw nothing in the street. Or did he? His heart started pounding when he spied a shadowy, cloaked figure in the moonlight. To his astonishment, the dark figure walked straight through the locked door of the bell tower and vanished. The thief rubbed his eyes. Strange.

He looked through the side window of the guardhouse and saw the policeman holding his gun cocked, eyes fixed on the belfry of the church. Above him the tower bells began to hum.

The thief's gaze returned to the moon-silhouetted tower. Arms prickling with fear, he watched heavy dark bells swaying slightly against the silver light of the moon. A dark figure stood among the bells, running a skeletal finger around the massive rim of the bell closest to the window. Then the dark shape started ringing the bells with its hands, ignoring the pull ropes. The muffled, melancholy tune bit right through the thief crouched beside the guardhouse. With each note, the thief felt an agonizing pain strike through his back and into his beating heart with stiletto sharpness.

The dark figure stepped to the edge of the tower, bells swaying behind it, and pointed a skeletal finger at the crouching thief. The thief gazed upward in horror as the hood fell back, revealing the face of the murdered bell ringer. The man's eyes were two points of fire, his skin withered and blackened as if overwhelmed by a scorching fire that burned just beneath the surface.

The thief felt the knife in his hand go white-hot, like a burning coal. The thief dropped the stiletto in panic and stared incredulously at the raw knife shape burned into his palm. Inside his pocket, the stolen keys grew red hot. He yelped in pain and saw them burning through the heavy cloth of his coat, wisps of smoke rising from the beleaguered garment. Then his whole torso was ablaze, and fire ran down from his coat toward his boots.

The thief screamed, but the sound was as muffled as the ringing of the bells above. He rolled frantically in the dirt, crying out to the policeman to come save him. But his voice did not carry beyond his own ears, and the engulfing flames burned hotter and hotter, no matter how hard he rolled.

The thief flung himself frantically down a side street, searching for water. There must be a stream nearby or a water butt. Something! Anything! The burning thief spied a water trough for horses behind a local inn and plunged into it, body ablaze. To his horror, the thief realized that the flames still burned brightly underneath the water. His hair and face were on fire. In crucifying agony, the thief heard his own skin sizzling, and the water in the trough began to boil.

Once again the thief heard his mother's voice in his head: "Honestly, that boy could get away with murder!" And he knew it wasn't true. Not then. Not now. Not ever again.

It was over in less than a minute. The water trough had boiled dry, and a small pile of ash lay at the bottom of a scorched, man-size hole. Back at the church the bells pealed loudly in triumph. Then they stopped ringing as abruptly as they started, and the dark figure in the tower vanished.

Inside the guardhouse, the policeman tore his eyes from the belfry and rubbed them with his free hand. Had he just seen what he thought he saw? How utterly bizarre.

A month after the murder of their beloved bell chief, the new head bell ringer brought a plain cardboard box to the minister. "I found this on a shelf in the belfry," he said. "It looks like someone made an anonymous donation to the church. Perhaps they want us to refurbish the bells?"

The minister's eyes widened in astonishment as he counted the cash inside the box. "How very generous!" he exclaimed. "I believe we have enough here to refurbish the lot, with some left over to buy a few more bells. Hallelujah!"

"Amen," said the head of the bell ringers.

14

The Baseball Game

BIRMINGHAM, AL

As soon as Uncle Henry heard about the big barbecue and baseball game in the next town, he was absolutely determined to go. Uncle Henry once pitched for the local team, and he still loved to see a good ball game. So, he got up early on Saturday morning and took the train down to the game.

Uncle Henry looked around until he found himself a good seat on one of the wagons lining the far end of the pasture where the barbecue and ball game were to take place. Pretty soon, the ballplayers came riding up on their big horses and crowded around the barbecue to get some food. There were a lot of people, and Uncle Henry had to fight his way through the laughing, arguing throng to get something to eat. The ballplayers had to rest for a bit under the big tree at the side of the field after eating too much barbecue. Then, as the spectators settled down with their food, the ballplayers started warming up on the field.

Uncle Henry reclaimed his spot on the wagon and ate with a good appetite. This was going to be a humdinger of a game, judging from the antics going on during the warm-up session. It was getting late, and Uncle Henry grew impatient. Why wasn't

THE BASEBALL GAME

the game starting? He asked a fellow what was happening and was told that one of the pitchers lived quite a ways out of town and hadn't arrived. A few minutes later, the pitcher rode up on his horse and ran out onto the field to warm up.

By the time the game started, it was late in the afternoon. Uncle Henry knew that he was going to miss the train back home if he stayed for the whole game, but it was so exciting that he just didn't care. He would walk home along the tracks.

What Uncle Henry hadn't planned on was the game going until it was nearly too dark to see. But what a game! It was tied right up until the very end, and then an unexpected home run decided the game in the home team's favor. Uncle Henry yelled himself hoarse with excitement.

And then it was over, and Uncle Henry realized he had to walk home in the dark. Uncle Henry never minded the long walk in the daytime, but walking the railroad tracks at night was not something he looked forward to. And how in tarnation was he going to see? At that moment, Uncle Henry spied a bottle on the ground beside the wagon, and he got an idea. He stopped at the local grocery store and bought enough kerosene to fill the bottle. Then he took off his necktie, folded it, and stuffed it into the bottle of kerosene like a wick. As soon as the tie was lit, Uncle Henry started walking down the railroad tracks toward home, using the bottle as a lantern to light his way.

The night got darker and darker. Storm clouds covered the sky, and Uncle Henry was getting mighty scared. He kept imagining that eyes were peering at him from beside the railroad tracks. Finally, Uncle Henry lost his nerve and started running as fast as his legs could carry him. Suddenly, a huge white dog with red eyes appeared, standing in the center of the tracks.

Uncle Henry stopped dead and stared at the dog. It seemed to grow larger and larger the longer he looked at it in the light from his bottle.

"Get back!" Uncle Henry shouted, waving the bottle at the dog. The necktie slipped out of the bottle and the light extinguished on the ground as the dog backed off a pace, its red eyes still glowing at Uncle Henry. Uncle Henry knew he was a goner. He ran for his life past the big white dog, hoping to get home before it could catch him. The big white dog ran after him, right on his heels, panting. Luckily, the dog's wild red eyes seemed to light the track so Uncle Henry did not stumble as he ran. Uncle Henry veered off the tracks when he got near home and ran through his neighbors' yards until he reached his own house. He didn't hear the dog chasing him anymore, and he collapsed on the front porch to try to catch his breath.

Aunt Jenny heard him fall onto the porch and came out with the lantern from the kitchen. When she saw him lying on the floorboards, she ran inside and brought him a dipper of well water. Uncle Henry drank it in one gulp and sat up. He drank two more dippers before he was ready to tell Aunt Jenny about the white dog chasing him all the way home.

When he finished his story, Aunt Jenny shook her head. "Uncle Henry, you're the strangest fellow I ever knew," she laughed at him. "That weren't an evil spirit, that was one of your friends come back from the grave to escort you home safely 'cause you stayed too long at that ball game."

Uncle Henry shook his head stubbornly. "Only reason I'm here is that I ran faster than that dog," he said.

He let Aunt Jenny pull him up, and she sat him down to a nice supper of collard greens, meat, and cracklin' bread.

The next morning, their next-door neighbor Jonathan stopped by to tell Uncle Henry and Aunt Jenny the latest news. The sheriff had caught two robbers lurking near the railroad tracks after the ball game.

"According to the sheriff," Jonathan said, "he's been trying to catch those thieves for a long while. They're always lurking near the tracks on ball game nights, waiting to rob people walking home from games. Sheriff says they're the ones that killed that fellow after the game last month. Lucky for everyone, the robbers were scared off by a big white dog near the train station last night, and the sheriff caught 'em."

"A white dog, did you say?" asked Aunt Jenny, glancing over at Uncle Henry, who had turned pale when he heard Jonathan's news.

"Yep. They were real scared of it. Told the sheriff it had red, glowing eyes and grew larger every time they looked at it. Guess the sheriff must have hit 'em too hard on the head," Jonathan said with a grin. "Well, I'd best pass the news along to the Smiths."

He hurried out the door on his way to the Smith house across the road. Aunt Jenny looked over at Uncle Henry as she closed the door behind him.

"You still think that white dog was an evil spirit?" she asked.

"No," Uncle Henry said, sitting down shakily on a chair.

"I think that white dog saved your life," Aunt Jenny said, sitting down opposite him. Uncle Henry nodded, speechless for once in his life.

"And you know what else I think?" asked Aunt Jenny. "I think you'd best get home before dark from now on."

"I think you're right," said Uncle Henry.

15

The Soldier's Ghost

LEE COUNTY, MS

It was late afternoon when I left my sweetheart's place for the long walk home. By the end of the second mile, I was dragging my tail, as my granny would say. Something I ate for supper disagreed with me, and my belly ached something awful. I wanted nothing more than some peppermint tea and a long sleep in my bed at home.

I'd just reached the old hunting trail that led to the other side of the low gap. It was a short cut that sliced nearly two miles off my trip, which sounded good to me. But I never used the trail at night because it was reputed to be haunted. I didn't want to be bothered with no ghosts, especially not with my belly a-rumbling and my head aching.

To heck with it, I decided. I felt so miserable, I wouldn't care if a haint came up and said "boo" right in my face. I just wanted to get home, quick.

The sun was setting with a spectacular display of oranges and reds when I reached the low gap. It was so pretty, I paused in spite of my rumbling tummy to watch for a moment.

Suddenly there was a sound like a ton of dynamite exploding. Something flew through the air and fell down on the trail about

THE SOLDIER'S GHOST

a hundred feet behind me. Boy howdy, that was not good. I jogged through the gap mighty quick and hastened down the trail. I don't know what made that sound or what it was that fell on the path, but it wasn't something I was going to look into tonight. No how, no way. I'd come back tomorrow in broad daylight and see what I could see then.

About a mile below the low gap, I realized something was following me. I could feel the hairs on my neck prickling as I sensed someone's eyes watching my every move. The figure behind me kept pace, even when I quickened my steps.

Alrighty then. I was no coward. If someone had something to say to me, they could say it to my dad-blame face. My tummy was aching, and my head was pounding, and I felt as sore as a bear with a toothache. I whipped around, ready to confront the person who was following me. To my astonishment, I saw a man wearing a Civil War soldier's uniform. Oh boy. The Civil War ended almost a hundred years ago. It was a haint. Not good.

The man stopped walking as soon as I turned around. His eyes were a funny reddish-brown color. They made my skin crawl.

Not wanting to appear frightened, I said: "You are a long way from home, soldier."

As soon as I opened my mouth, the haint's eyes started glowing like they were on fire. He rose several inches from the ground and came swooping toward me, his arms extended like he was going to grab me and carry me away.

I hit the ground hard, rolling off the path into the bushes, and the haint flew over my head with a cry of rage. He was flying so fast that he crossed all the way over to the far side of the hill a hundred yards away.

I jumped to my feet, lickety-split, and ran as fast as my legs would carry me toward the creek at the bottom of the incline. Haints couldn't cross running water, so I knew I'd be safe if I could get there before that ghost got himself turned around.

I could hear that haint close behind me. His ghostly body was buzzing like a swarm of bees, and the red glow from his eyes lit up my path. I was only a yard ahead of the haint when I reached the creek. I threw myself down the bank and tumbled into the running water, my bottom landing on a sharp rock. I looked up and saw the phantom pull up sharply, repelled by the running water. With a scream that chilled my blood, it rose up and up into the sky, burning so bright I had to close my eyes against the glare. Then it vanished, and the holler went dark around me.

I fell back onto the pebbles of the creek, gasping for air as water splashed over my shaking body. My heart was a-pounding like a hammer on an anvil, and I turned over and lost my supper. I was never so grateful for water in my whole durned life.

When I was sure it was safe, I ran for home like a frightened babe looking for its mama. I built up a big fire in the hearth and sat so close to it my hair got singed. I drank several cups of peppermint tea while I dripped myself dry. Then I went to bed, cursing all ghosts and haints and tummy aches from here to Sunday and back.

I never took that shortcut home again, day or night. One haint was plenty enough for me.

PART TWO
Powers of Darkness and Light

16

Vampire Hermit

She was nervous, and she did not know why. It was a perfect place for them to stay for the season—an old, abandoned house where a hermit once lived. Perhaps she was spooked at the idea of sharing the house with a corpse, for the body of the hermit lay enshrined in a birch-bark coffin in the loft. It was an old custom and one no longer popular among her people, for which she was thankful. But the hermit had a reputation for being odd, and when he insisted on staying in his home after his death, the folks from the nearby village had done as he wished.

The house was open to any who wanted to stay there, and hunters sometimes spent the night. But the women in the nearby village had warned her against stopping there with her baby daughter. The house had a strange reputation, and the hermit himself had told the women of the village to stay away.

She told her young husband what the village women had said, but he only laughed at the gossip. There was good hunting here, her man had declared; soon they would prosper, and he could build a better home for her and their baby daughter. So they traveled along the footpaths until they came to the hermit's house, and they unpacked their few belongings in the

Vampire Hermit

front room. She would not, she told her husband, go up into the loft where the hermit's body lay in its birch-bark coffin. Her husband teased her for being cowardly but could not change her mind.

Her husband left the house soon afterward to hunt. She immediately put her daughter in the sling on her back and went to look for roots and berries. They would make a nice addition to whatever her husband killed for supper, she reasoned, although her real purpose was to get out of the hermit's house. She stayed away until her husband returned with the meat, and then went inside to prepare the evening meal for them. Her husband yawned and stretched, tired from his hunting, and climbed up into the loft to rest.

The hut soon filled with the delicious smell of roasting meat. She was sorting through the berries when she heard a muffled cry and the very final-sounding crunch of breaking bones. She stiffened in shock and was about to call out, but some instinct stopped her. As she stared upward, frozen in horror, blood started to drip from the rafters above the place her husband had lain down to sleep. She heard sounds of gnawing and slurping coming from the loft overhead.

On the pretext of getting something from one of the packs, she crept silently to the far corner of the room where she could see up into the loft. A skeleton with glowing red eye sockets was perched on the legs of her dead husband. Its teeth and chin were covered with blood, as if it had been feasting on his body.

She crept back out of view before the skeleton saw her and was quietly sick in the corner. Her daughter stirred restlessly at her back, and she knew she had to get away immediately or she and her child would be killed too.

"I am going to run down to the stream to fetch water for the broth," she called toward the loft. "I will be right back." She took the pail and walked carelessly toward the stream, trying to appear normal. As soon as she was out of sight among the trees, she started to run as fast as she could, back along the footpaths to the nearest village. The baby bounced and bumped in the sling. Not liking the jarring movements, her infant daughter began to cry. Her wails were answered by a terrible howl from the direction of the house. The evil creature had just realized they were escaping.

The young mother ran as fast as she could through the darkening woods. She could hear the creature's howls growing closer as it pursued them, and she increased her speed, tearing off one of her scarves and throwing it down for the skeleton to maul. She heard the trees rustling behind her, and then the sounds of pursuit stopped for a moment as the beast pounced on her scarf and tore it to bits in its fury. She kept running, her little daughter wailing desperately as she sensed her mother's fear.

Each time she heard the creature drawing close to her, the young mother threw off another scarf for it to savage, until she had none left. Then she threw off her moccasins, one after the other, to buy them more time. She was sobbing exhaustedly and was nearly without hope. Her infant was clinging to her hair, too scared even to cry as they fled through the darkness. She could hear the monster gaining on her, and she had nothing left to shed save the few items keeping her decent enough to enter the village.

The creature's howls were very close now, and she knew she couldn't run much farther. She could see the lights from the village through the trees in front of her, though it was still far off. In a last act of despair, she cried for help, hoping someone would be near enough to hear it. To her joy, her call was taken up by women's voices from just outside the wall of the village and answered by the hunters from within. The creature was so close now she could hear it breathing, and she summoned the last of her strength and sprinted to the trees at the edge of the village. Here her strength failed her, and she collapsed to the ground, her little daughter wailing in terror.

Before the monster could pounce on them, a party of hunters burst through the gates of the village. The creature leaped back into the trees as the men surrounded her, searching left and right for her attacker. They swung their torches wide when they glimpsed a figure in the trees, and the skeleton retreated farther into the woods. The young mother lay gasping and sobbing on the ground, too spent to speak. Realizing that it had lost its prey, the creature called to the young mother: "Today the luck was yours. We will see what tomorrow brings."

Then it was gone. The hunters carried the young mother into the village. The women came to tend to her and her child, while the hunters stood guard over them throughout the night. The next morning the woman told the chief her story, and the hunters went immediately to the hermit's house to search for the creature that had tried to kill her. They found her husband dead in the loft of the house, his neck broken and a gaping hole in his side. In the birch-bark coffin, the mouth of the hermit's skeleton was covered with the young man's blood.

Enraged at this act of vampirism, the hunters set fire to the cabin. As the flames encompassed the house, a terrible howling and roaring came from the loft. Men were posted at each exit, but a long, low figure leaped through the flames and jumped out the back window. It looked like a jackrabbit, but its howls were not human. It dodged the weapons thrown at it and escaped between the legs of two hunters. The creature disappeared into the woods, and though the men pursued, they did not catch it. But the vampire had lost its human shape and its powers; it did not come again to plague the young woman or her daughter.

The Minstrel

WILKES-BARRE, PA

I spent fifty years down in the mines before my strength gave out and my hands got too crippled with arthritis to work. I was proud of that accomplishment. Not many men live to old age working in a coal mine.

I've lived my whole life in a "mine patch"—that's what we miners called our mining communities. The communities

THE MINSTREL

and all the folks in them were owned by the coal companies, body and soul. I was brought into the world by a company doctor, and when I go out of it someday, I'll be buried in a company cemetery. Churches, stores, and schools are all owned by the Coal King—that's what we call our absentee owner. I know one fellow who had the following epitaph carved on his tombstone: "Forty years with pick and drill / Down in the coal to pay my bills. / The Coal King's slave, by now I've passed / Hallelujah, I'm free at last!"

When I was a child, everyone living and working in the mine patches came from Scotland or Wales. Things changed, sometime around 1880, and the patches filled up with miners from all over the world. Suddenly, we were working side by side with Slavs, Germans, Hungarians, Italians, and some ex-slaves whose ancestors came from Africa. It was an odd mix of folks, and it took a while for things to settle down in the patches. There was a lot of fighting and tension, but as our supervisor used to say, "The coal you dig ain't Slav or Pole or Irish coal. It's just coal." And he was right.

The one thing that made life bearable for us all was music. We were surrounded by song and poetry all day long. Mine workers sang in the branch entries deep below the ground while waiting for the dust and smoke to settle in their "rooms" after they blasted down the coal. Mule drivers sang and joked during the long rides through the mine. Song followed song at the barroom on payday; sometimes the families of the miners would gather under a moonlit sky with the tower colliery building and culm banks in the background, and we would sing and tell stories, and dance the night away to the smell of coal dust and brimstone. We'd pull out a plate of sheet iron borrowed from the colliery and use it for a dance floor as a fiddler scraped out tune after lively tune. Irishmen would dance with Italian women, and Slav miners mixed with Poles, forgetting their differences for a time.

There were some men among us who were born minstrels, lads who could dramatize a song with the lift of an eyebrow or the gesture of one hand. These men were the soul of the mining patch. They came and went in the manner of the bards of old, traveling to and fro among the patches in the county. Those whose feet were too restless would walk over the whole of anthracite coal country, singing for their meals and bringing delight to all the coal men and their families.

I was a young man when I first met Nathaniel Kramer, who was a fiddler and a minstrel and a pretty good blacksmith when he set his mind that way. Nat had a voice that was so sweet it could charm the birds, and a manner that was so funny that he had the most hard-core miner rolling on the floor with tears streaming down his cheeks. A whole bunch of us were sitting on the porch of the company store one day when Nat came strolling up the road with his fiddle. He set his case down on the ground, put his fiddle under his chin, and started to sing: "Winter or the summertime / Whether rain or whether shine / Every man is there in line / Seated on the step." He gestured to us with his bow, and we laughed aloud, because there we all were, sitting on the steps of the porch, like always. We liked this new minstrel at once and settled back to wait for more.

Seeing the bright expectation in our faces, Nat scraped away at the fiddle again and sang a sly song about Neddy Kearn's brand-new shovel that was broken by Barney Gallagher down in the coal mine. Well, the fistfight that followed this minor tragedy was tremendous! The other miners gathered 'round to cheer the combatants on, and Neddy Kearn had just about clobbered poor old Barney Gallagher when the mine boss came in and broke up the fight. Nat finished with a wink and a shake of his head, all that fuss and bother "was all about the shovel that was broke in two!" To a man, we rose to our feet on the steps of the company porch and applauded until our hands were sore.

That was the beginning of a lifelong friendship between me and Nat Kramer. He fiddled at my wedding to Cynthia O'Malley, the prettiest girl who ever lived in a mine patch, and he sang special ballads at the christenings of our three daughters and two sons. In return, we always kept a place by the fire for Nat and a warm room for him to sleep in whenever he came to town.

Sometimes, Nat would slip in late at night after we had all gone to bed. Whenever we heard him arrive, the whole family would creep from our beds, gather around the kitchen fireplace, and listen to him fiddle until the dawn. On those nights, Nat would sing to us about the life of the coal miner—about our life—the only life we had ever known.

> *Down in a coal mine, underneath the ground,*
> *Where a gleam of sunshine never can be found;*
> *Digging dusky diamonds all the year around,*
> *Away down in a coal mine, underneath the ground.*
> *At every shift, be it soon or late, I haste my bread to earn,*
> *And anxiously my kindred wait and watch for my return;*
> *For death that levels all alike, whate'er their rank may be,*
> *Amid the fire and damp may strike and fling his darts at me.*

There came a day when an explosion trapped me and some of the lads in a shaft for a night and a day. The air was going bad, and I thought it was the end for me. I wasn't afraid for myself; there was no pain. Death would be like falling asleep, with heaven on the other side. But I hated to leave Cynthia and the children with so little. I was nearly asleep when a bright light pierced my eyelids. I looked up into the faces of the mine boss and my old friend Nat, who had come down into the mine to help dig me out. I gulped desperate, deep breaths of the clean air and cried like a baby as they pulled me and the other men out of the shaft and into blessed freedom and life.

We were the lucky ones. Only a few decades ago, there was a fire in the Avondale mine that caused a major tragedy. Nat must have read my mind, because he gave me a broad smile and started softly humming the tune of the Avondale Mine Disaster: "A hundred and ten of brave strong men were smothered underground; / They're in their graves till the last day, their widows may bewail / And the orphans' cries they rend the skies all around through Avondale." But there was no disaster on this day. There was only light, and laughter, and within an hour the feel of my wife's arms around me, holding me tight.

Fifty years came and went in a flash, and one special night I found myself sitting in a chair of honor out in the old field under a moonlit sky with the tower colliery building and culm banks in the background. It was my birthday and the day I retired permanently from the coal mine. With me were my loving family: my coal-mining sons and my beautiful daughters, my wonderful grandchildren, and a great-gran or two as well. One or two old friends had survived the mines and were sitting at the head table with me on this great day, and many of the new friends I had made over the years were there as well, celebrating my good fortune.

The youngsters were already dancing to the smell of coal dust and brimstone on the plate of sheet iron we'd borrowed from the colliery as several fiddlers and guitar players scraped out a merry tune, singing ballad after ballad. It was a time to rejoice. A coal miner had made it out of the mine with his life intact and—more rare even than this—some money in his pocket to retire on. Cynthia sat next to me, holding my hand tight and smiling through her tears.

I kept looking around for one face in particular. Finally, I leaned over to Cynthia and asked, "Where's Nat?"

Cynthia looked troubled. "I sent the word out a month ago that we wanted him to come and play at your birthday/retirement party," she said. "You know how hard he is to track down when he is wandering. I'm sure he will be here. He wouldn't let anything stand in the way of his attending your party."

I nodded my head. What she said was true. Nat would come to the party.

It was very late when the impromptu band stopped playing and a voice rang out over the crowd.

"A happy birthday to you, Terry Jenkins, and congratulations on your retirement!"

Nat stood at the head of the iron dance floor with a glass of beer in his hand. The crowd echoed his words and drank a toast to my health. I stood and bowed low in response to the toast, while around me all my family and friends applauded and cheered. Then Nat took out his fiddle and began to play "The Old Miner's Refrain" for me.

Where are the boys that worked with me in the breakers long ago?
Many of them now have gone to rest;
Their cares of life are over, and they've left this world of woe,
And their spirits now are roaming with the blest.

When he finished the song, the entire field erupted into applause, and tears were surreptitiously wiped from many eyes. I went over to the dance floor and gave Nat a bear hug, filled with love and gratitude for this old friend of mine. To my surprise, his clothes were damp and smelled of dirt and mildew. Looking closer, I saw that his eyes were red-rimmed, and his face was far too pale for my liking.

"Old friend, you don't look well," I said, as I pulled back from our hug.

Then Nat said something strange: "I had to come back this once, Terry. Just for you. I'll see you on the other side."

With a sad, sweet smile, Nat walked away into the darkness. I watched him go, knowing in my bones that it was the last time I would ever see him. Cynthia must have seen a shadow cross my face, for she came over and took my hand.

"I told you he would come," she whispered to me. "He loves you like a brother."

I nodded sadly, then forced myself to smile as I turned back to the party.

I didn't want to spoil Cynthia's evening, so I waited until the next day to tell her what Nat had said. "He must be sick," Cynthia concluded when I finished my story. "We should try to find him. He should stay here with the family that loves him during his last days."

She got up from the kitchen table with a look of determination and went over to the wall telephone. Cranking the handle a few times, she called the operator and asked to be put through to Scranton, which was always Nat's next stop on his circuit after Wilkes-Barre. Our eldest grandson was living and working in Scranton at the time, and Nat usually went to stay with him. Joshua and his wife had missed my birthday party last night because their new baby was ill, so Cynthia had to give him a full update on the party before she could bring up Nat Kramer.

I was listening with only half an ear while I whittled a fancy toy horse for my newest great-gran. But I knew my wife's voice well, and I looked up quickly when a note of fear and alarm entered it.

"What?" Cynthia said. "Are you sure? But he was here last night, I swear. Everyone saw him, heard him play! Terry gave him a hug just before he left."

I hurried to my wife's side. "What is it?" I asked, loudly enough so that my grandson could hear my question over the phone. Cynthia covered the receiver with her hand.

"Joshua says that Nat Kramer is dead. He died of pneumonia last week and was buried in the churchyard near their home."

I sat down hard on the nearest chair, remembering the smell of wet dirt and mildew that had clung to Nat's clothes, remembering his pale face and his parting words. Cynthia was remembering them, too.

"Dear God in heaven," she gasped, the phone slipping from her grasp. She sank to the floor, her head between her knees. We could hear our grandson calling out frantically to us over the phone, but neither of us had the strength to answer him. Finally, I drew in a deep breath, took up the phone again, reassured Joshua that we would call him back, and hung up the receiver. Then I sat down on the floor beside my wife of more than forty years and took her hand in mine.

"You were right, Cynthia," I said finally. "Nat didn't let anything stand in the way of his coming to my party. Not even death."

He must have risen out of his grave very early that morning and walked all the way to Wilkes-Barre with his fiddle in order to play me one last song. I leaned my head back against the wall, suddenly overwhelmed by the love that had prompted such devotion to a lifelong friend. I felt tears rolling down my cheeks, and I could do nothing to check them. Cynthia clung to me, laughing and crying and completely spooked by such an uncanny ending to our friendship with Nathaniel Kramer.

"Though it's not really an ending," I told her when I had calmed down again. "Remember what Nat said. He would see me on the other side."

"And so he will." Cynthia spoke confidently. "Someday."

18

Flaming Reflection

CHILLICOTHE, OH

It was a chilly Friday morning in February 1918 when I first heard about the "magic" mirror. The six-year-old granddaughter of a local family had seen a "bad-looking man" in their looking glass, which faced a blank wall. The girl had glanced into the mirror and screamed with fright. When her father and grandfather gazed into the glass, they saw a woman holding a baby in her arms. None of the figures in the glass were present in the dining room when they appeared in the mirror.

People were talking about the incident all over town, so I wasn't surprised when my next-door neighbor dropped by to discuss the phenomenon. According to Susan, people were flocking to the house to look into the "magic" mirror. All kinds of visions were showing up: bodiless faces of strangers, deceased loved ones, old men with gray whiskers, women holding infants. One fellow saw a horse's head with a flowing mane. The vision was different for each person.

"The pictures don't have any color. They appear black and white and gray," Susan said, sipping her second cup of tea. "You know, the family will let anyone look in their mirror. I think we should try it."

Flaming Reflection

I considered the matter. My family treated mirrors with caution and I'd picked up the habit from them. My parents only had one mirror in their house, though it was a fancy mirror with lots of symbols carved into the wooden frame. My grandparents' lone mirror was a perfect copy of my parents.' And we only had one mirror in the washroom, though ours lacked a fancy frame.

I once asked my grandmother why the family disliked mirrors. "You shouldn't put stock in outward appearances," she said crisply. This made no sense to me. Why did she own a fancy mirror if she didn't put stock in "outward appearances?" Grandmother refused to speak further on the matter, so I let it be.

I decided it probably wouldn't do me any harm to try the Chillicothe mirror, so Susan, her married daughter, and I drove across town to see what we would see. It seemed like half the town had crowded into the house, hoping for a look in the dining room mirror. As we waited, other visitors excitedly told us that three different deputy sheriffs had come to run tests, but they were unable to explain the mystery.

When our turn came, Susan went first. She gazed into the mirror in the flickering light of the gas-lamps. "I see a man," she said, her voice sounding awed. "He has a halo around his head. He looks like Saint Christopher!"

Her daughter was next. She stared for a long time into the glass. "All I see is the wall," she said sadly.

My pulse jumped with excitement as I sat down before the mirror. I focused my attention on the blank wall, as instructed. Almost immediately, gray fog swirled in the glass. My heart hammered with excitement. What would I see? Then the glass burst into flames. A pair of malevolent dark eyes glared out at me. I screamed and leapt to my feet, toppling the chair. I put my hand over my mouth and ran out of the room. Those wicked eyes—they wanted to kill me. And I'd felt heat pouring out of the glass.

"I don't want to talk about it," I mumbled to my neighbor when Susan asked what happened. One look at my face silenced her. When we reached home, I quietly thanked my neighbor and let myself into the house with shaking hands. My husband was there before me, heating soup on the burner. He took one look and hurried over to clasp me in his arms. "What happened?" he asked.

I told him everything. His face was grim when I finished. "That family is messing around with the occult," he said.

"Are they?" I whispered. "Susan saw a saint in the mirror. That doesn't sound occult. Maybe it's me. Something about me drew that . . . that thing to the mirror."

My husband scoffed, but every instinct I possessed told me that I was right.

I avoided the mirror in the washroom that night. Supposedly the phenomenon only happened when the mirror faced a blank wall, but I wasn't willing to risk it.

A good night's sleep allayed my fears. My husband was right. It was the strange mirror that caused my scary vision. It had nothing to do with me. I wandered sleepily into the washroom and used the facilities. Then I stepped to the sink to wash my hands and glanced into the mirror. And saw dark, malevolent eyes in a woman's burning face stare hatefully into mine. I shrieked and fell over, landing untidily on the rug. My husband came running, sure I had injured myself. I panted with fear, tears streaming unheeded down my face. "She was there! In the mirror," I wept.

"Who was there?" he asked.

"The fiery woman with the evil eyes."

To his credit, he believed me. He hugged me tight until I calmed down. Then he said, "Let's experiment and see what happens."

I gaped at him. He took both my hands in his. "I want to know the extent of this . . . haunting. I'm going to look in the mirror. Let's see if the woman appears."

He stood up and looked into the mirror. Nothing happened.

"All right. Now you stand up behind me and look in the mirror," he instructed.

I gulped in fear. But he was right. We needed to know what we were facing. I stood up. The woman's face was instantly there, writhed in flames. A hand with razor-sharp nails flashed out of the glass, striking at me. My husband knocked it away and the claws ripped his cheek as he tumbled both of us to the floor out of the creature's reach. The evil visage nodded toward the window. The curtain caught fire. Swearing, my husband grabbed a towel and beat out the flames. The figure in the mirror smiled with satisfaction and vanished.

"Dear God in heaven," my husband muttered. We mopped up the wounds on his face and were removing the scorched curtain from the rod when the phone rang. It was far too early in the morning for callers, but the phone blared insistently. Taking my hand, my husband led us downstairs to answer it. When the operator put the call through, he heard my grandmother's voice say, "You must come here immediately, before she gets out." The line went dead.

"Your grandmother is some kind of spiritualist, isn't she?" my husband asked as he hung up the phone.

"She calls herself a faith healer," I responded. "I think this is the reason no one in my family likes mirrors."

"Yes, indeed," my husband replied. He fingered the bloody scratches on his cheek. We hurried out to the car and drove straight to my grandparents' place.

Grandmother was pegging clothes to the wash line when we arrived. She dropped the bag of clothespins into the laundry basket and came to meet us. Her eyes narrowed when she saw the slashes on my husband's cheek.

"Come inside," she said, and led us through the side door into the kitchen.

Granddad put a mug of coffee into my husband's hand and gave me a peck on the cheek. "Sylvie said you were having a mess of trouble at your place," he remarked, sitting down at the kitchen table. He tapped the newspaper in front of him, which described the fuss over the Chillicothe mirror.

"You went there yesterday, didn't you?" Grandmother asked, rinsing her hands at the sink. "I felt her wake up and knew you'd looked into that mirror."

"I wish you'd explain what is going on. Who is she? Why is she haunting me?" I asked the questions a bit more forcefully than I realized and drew a deep breath, trying to calm down.

"She's a witch who was burned to death many years ago by a mob when they discovered that she was stealing the lives and the youth from the girl-children in their town," Grandmother said calmly. "Folks at that time called her Bloody Mary. You are a direct descendant of the man who stopped her. Upon her death, her spirit was trapped in her magic mirror. She is still seeking vengeance against our family. That's why we bind all our mirrors against her. Even then, sometimes her spirit is too strong for the binding, and she bursts forth into the living world, wreaking havoc wherever she goes."

"Like clawing people's faces and setting fire to curtains?" my husband asked dryly.

"Much worse than that," said my grandmother. "She killed my younger brother."

Dear God. I sank onto a kitchen chair and took the cup of coffee Granddad thrust into my hand. It was a bit much to take in all at once.

"When it became apparent that the witch's spirit was haunting our family, our ancestors started studying the old ways to learn how to keep it at bay," Grandmother continued. "One person each generation is given special instruction in these matters and certain artifacts are entrusted to them. I am the guardian for my generation. Your father will be the next guardian. We weren't sure which of you grandchildren would follow your father. It might have been one of your cousins. But after yesterday, I think it is you."

"I wish you had told me," I said, putting the coffee mug down on the table. "I wouldn't be in this mess. What do we do now?"

"We bind her spirit anew," Grandmother said.

"That sounds simple," I said ironically.

My husband grinned appreciatively and poured another cup of coffee.

Over the next two days, I had a crash course in spiritualism, spending every waking moment at my grandparents' house learning prayers and chants and rituals while Grandmother and my father—called in to help—prepared the ground. The once mirrorless house now boasted three ornate-looking glasses, covered with burlap, as well as sacred candles, a bell, holy water, and other ritual items.

The binding ceremony would take place in three parts, and the first part was mine. My husband was allowed to accompany me, but he couldn't participate. I took his hand and led him upstairs to the third-floor attic.

The covered floor-mirror stood in the center of a chalked symbol. My husband stood next to the door praying as I lit the candles and took my place in front of the mirror. Chanting the words my grandmother taught me, I reached out and pulled the burlap off the mirror, tossing it outside the chalked outline on the floor. The glass writhed with gray fog and then started to burn. Scorching heat pressed out at me as a woman's twisted face formed in the mirror. I chanted and rang my bell once, twice. She threw herself toward me and banged hard against the glass. The thud shook the attic and my husband tensed, ready to spring to my rescue. The heat was unbearable. My skin was sizzling as I shouted the last words and rang my bell a third time.

From the floor below, I heard my father's voice raised in prayer. The woman hammering against the glass paused and looked behind her. She vanished and I knew she had flung herself into the mirror below, trying to reach my father. I uttered the final words of this portion of the ritual, lifted the chalice of holy water from the table beside me and poured it over the mirror. The flames flickered out. The fog cleared and I could see myself reflected in the mirror.

The floor below me shook, and I knew my father and the witch were fighting. I carefully stepped out of the chalked figure and walked down to the ground floor. All three of us were needed for the final binding.

My father's voice rose to a shout, and an almighty bang shook the whole house. I heard my grandmother's voice in the front parlor, intoning the words of the third chant. My father joined my husband and I in the front hallway. Father was sweating profusely but unhurt. I returned my attention to the front room. I could see my grandmother through the partially open door, and the heat from the ornate mirror before her was so intense that we felt it in the hallway. The power and intensity of the fight between my grandmother and the witch made my hair stand on end.

"The room is on fire," my husband said in a too-calm voice, picking up one of the water buckets that lined the hallway. Granddad stood ready with another as Grandmother shouted a long string of syllables in a language long forgotten. This was our cue. Father took my hand and together we stepped into the flaming front parlor. My skin sizzled and the pain was intense, but we staggered forward until we stood on either side of my grandmother. The three of us joined hands and chanted together. Every word burnt my lips, my tongue, my throat. There was no way I was going to survive this, I thought grimly. But I let this creature out and I would die with dignity binding her anew.

An acrid red cloud burst from the mirror, encompassing the three of us. We choked on the bitter smoke but managed to shout a final word of binding. A blinding white light filled the room, pushing the red cloud back toward the mirror. The pressure was so intense I thought my body would explode. The whole house shook and we fell to the floor. The heat abruptly ceased. I lay for a moment, light-blinded and shaking. When my eyes slowly cleared, I saw that the room looked completely normal—no fire, no scorch marks. Not a stick of furniture was out of place. Beside us, the mirror was simply a mirror. But Grandmother, Father, and I were covered with black soot from head to toe. And I had the worst sunburn of my life.

"Is she gone?" I asked, my voice hoarse.

"Yes," said my exhausted grandmother.

"Will she come back?" I asked, my voice tiny and frightened.

"Yes," said Father. "But not today."

Granddad and my husband burst into the room and pulled us carefully to our feet. Hugs would have to wait until our burned skin had healed.

It took two weeks for my sunburn to clear up. I could barely stand the feel of sheets on my body for the first couple of nights. But everything was all right now. Our washroom mirror had a fancy new frame with ritual symbols carved into it, ensuring our continued safety. Thank God.

I learned later that the authorities asked the Chillicothe family to stop letting people use their "magic" mirror. Which was just as well. Who knows what else might try to escape from such a mirror? In my opinion, it was best to put it where no one could use it again.

19

Wait Until Emmett Comes

CHARLESTON, WV

There's a story I heard once about a preacher who was riding home from a visit with several poor folks in his parish when darkness fell. It was about to storm and the only shelter around was an old, abandoned mansion, reputed to be haunted. The preacher clutched his Bible and said, "The Lord will take care of me."

The preacher arrived at the mansion just as the storm broke. He put his horse in the barn and made his way to the house. The preacher walked across the rotten old porch and tried the front door. It was unlocked. When he ventured through the creaky portal, he found himself in a wide entrance hall liberally strewn with dusty cobwebs. He glanced at his reflection in a large, cracked mirror with an ornate gold frame and straightened his cap. Then he caught a glimpse of another room opening off the entrance hall full of sheet-covered furniture. In the dimness of twilight, the sheets looked like ghosts, and the preacher gave a muffled shriek of alarm before realizing what they were.

The preacher was mighty glad there wasn't anyone there to hear his silly yell. To prove to himself that he wasn't scared of haunts, he walked through the downstairs rooms, looking

WAIT UNTIL EMMETT COMES

in shadowy corners, underneath shrouded furniture, and inside empty bookcases. To his relief, the preacher didn't find a single haunt on the main floor.

The preacher retraced his steps to a large sitting room that he had found during his explorations. It stood at the end of a long passageway, and an enormous fireplace filled one entire wall. Coal for a fire had already been laid out, and several comfortable chairs were grouped invitingly around the hearth. The preacher thought it was the perfect place to wait out the storm. It was quite a surprise to find such a pleasant room in an abandoned mansion, but the preacher did not question this happenstance. He just went inside and lit the coal fire. Then he settled down in one of the comfortable chairs and began to read his Bible. The fire smoldered in a heap of glowing coals as the storm howled around the mansion and shook the windows. *It was really a terrible night to be outside*, the preacher thought. He had made the right choice, stopping here for the evening. Imagine trying to ride home in this rain! The preacher put a few more coals on the fire and sat back with a sigh of contentment.

More than an hour had passed in this pleasant manner when the preacher was roused from his reading by a strange noise. He looked up from his Bible and saw a very large black cat stretching itself in the doorway. The black cat strolled over to the fireplace and sat down among the red-hot coals. The preacher swallowed nervously as the cat picked up a coal in its paw and licked it. Then the cat got up, shook itself, and walked to the foot of the preacher's chair. It fixed its blazing yellow eyes on the preacher, black tail lashing, and said quietly, "Wait until Emmett comes."

The preacher gasped. He had never heard of a talking cat before.

The black cat sat down in front of the preacher and watched him without blinking. When nothing else happened, the preacher turned back to his Bible, nervously muttering to himself, "The Lord will take care of me."

A few minutes later, another cat came into the room. It was black as midnight and as large as the biggest dog you've ever seen. It strolled over to the fireplace, laid down among the red-hot coals, and lazily batted them with its enormous paws. Then it walked over to the first cat and said, "Shall we do it now?"

The first cat replied, "Let's wait until Emmett comes."

The two black cats sat facing the chair, watching as the preacher read through the Pauline Epistles at top speed. Their blazing yellow eyes seemed never to blink.

A breeze swirled through the sitting room, rustling the black cats' fur and tangling the preacher's hair. The air grew colder and colder, dampening the warmth of the fire and the cheery crackling of the flames. A third black cat, big as a panther, entered the room. It went to the enormous fireplace full of red-hot coals and rolled among them, chewing some and spitting them out. Then it ambled over to the other two black cats that were facing the preacher in his chair.

"What shall we do with him?" it growled to the others.

"We should not do anything until Emmett comes," the black cats replied together.

The preacher flipped to Revelation, looking fearfully around the room. Then he snapped shut his Bible and stood up.

"Goodnight cats," he said politely. "I'm glad of your company, but when Emmet comes, you tell him I've been here . . . and gone!"

20

Mothman

They were too excited to go straight home after the prom, so the group headed to the local Soda Shoppe to drink root beer floats and flirt with their dates. Natalie was thrilled to be out late on this special night, in spite of the dreary rain that threatened to frizz her hair. Her prom date, Alex, was captain of the football team and considered the best catch in school. Natalie had won a lot of popularity points when he'd asked her to be his date at the prom.

When the root beer floats arrived, Tim—who was dating Natalie's friend Annie—leaned forward and waggled his eyebrows at the two girls. "I hear the Mothman has been seen just outside town," he said in a frightening voice, "waiting to pounce on pretty girls and eat their hearts out."

"Ha, ha. Very funny," Annie said with a frown.

Natalie frowned in confusion. "Who is the Mothman?" she asked. Natalie had moved to town at the beginning of the school year and still didn't know all the local legends.

Tim and Alex were happy to fill her in on the Mothman. As they sipped their sodas, the boys told Natalie the following legend.

MOTHMAN

There was once a scientist who worked on top-secret government projects at a local chemical plant during World War II. The scientist was developing a chemical weapon from the poison of South American moths that would destroy the enemy and bring a rapid end to the war. He worked long hours, late into the night, and grew so tired that he started making mistakes. One night the beaker where he brewed his deadly concoctions exploded right in his face. The scientist was blown through the wall of his office and lay on the floor of the hallway, writhing in desperate pain as chemicals burned through his body. As the top-secret potion mixed with the scientist's body chemicals, the man started mutating. Great mothlike wings burst from his shoulder blades; his arms and legs elongated; claws formed on his fingers and toes; and his eyes glowed red with fire. His incisors became fangs that bit right through his lips, tearing them to shreds. The mutated scientist licked hungrily at the blood with his striped tongue, and the taste awakened another fire in his gut—a deep, burning desire for human flesh.

The accident in the lab had triggered the alarm bell. Night watchmen ran into the hallway and came face-to-face with the new monster. They were the first to die. One man escaped into a guard booth and called in another alarm while the monster tore at the door with superhuman strength. The guard's frantic babbling was cut off by a sudden scream as the monster tore out his heart with its sharp claws. His dying words were: "Mothman. Save us from the Mothman." The phone dropped from his lifeless hand as the newly christened Mothman sank down on its haunches and devoured the man's dripping heart, chuckling in delight as blood spattered its twisted face. By the time the police arrived, the monster had vanished into the mountainous forest behind the chemical factory

"The Mothman is still out there, waiting for unsuspecting people to walk in the woods so he can eat their hearts," Tim concluded gleefully.

Natalie shuddered. She couldn't help it. Alex laughed and threw his arm over her shoulders. "Why don't I drive Natalie home, so she feels safe," he said. "You and Annie can wait for the bill, right, Tim?"

Alex tossed his buddy some cash and hustled Natalie out of the Soda Shoppe with a broad wink. Natalie heard Annie giggling. They both knew why Tim and Alex had told such a scary story. The boys thought the girls would be ready to do some snuggling after receiving such a scare. And Natalie had to admit, the idea of cuddling with Alex was very appealing. He was really cute!

Natalie wasn't surprised when Alex pulled off onto a remote country road about halfway home and proposed parking for a while. She blushed demurely and agreed. Just as Alex slipped his arm around her, the car shook from front to back, as if struck by a mighty wind. Natalie gave a small shriek and clutched his shirt in alarm. "What was that?" she cried. "Was it the Mothman?"

Alex laughed. "Relax, darling. It's just a thunderstorm." He pulled her close.

"I'm scared," Natalie said. She thought she had seen a dark shadow pass over the car just after the wind shook it. In her mind, she pictured a twisted face with fangs eating the security guard's bleeding heart.

"Relax, babe," Alex said and kissed her. Alex was a good kisser. Natalie forgot her fear and kissed him back.

Suddenly, the whole vehicle rocked on its wheels as something large landed on the roof with a huge thump. Natalie pulled away from Alex with a shriek.

"What was that?"

"The wind just knocked a branch onto the roof," Alex said, trying to kiss her again.

"I want to go home," Natalie said, her voice trembling with fear.

A high-pitched whine came from the roof. It sounded like claws were scraping the metal. Natalie screamed. "The Mothman is here! Alex, I want to go home."

"It's just the tree branch scratching the top of the car," Alex said. "Come on, Natalie. We never have time to ourselves. Just ignore it."

But Natalie was too scared to stay. "Take me home, Alex," she repeated stubbornly.

"Look, if it makes you happy, I will pull the branch off the car," Alex said, hopping out into the rain before Natalie could protest. He stuck his head back in the door and said, "Lock the door behind me if it makes you feel better. I'll knock when I've got the branch off the car."

Natalie locked the door behind Alex and sat listening to the rain thudding against the car as Alex disappeared into the darkness. She heard a sudden thump overhead, and the car rocked a third time. That must have been Alex pulling the branch off the roof. The car rocked once more, and a puff of wind rattled the windows. Then everything grew still save the gentle patter of the rain. One minute passed and then two. Natalie shivered and rubbed the goose bumps on her arms as she waited for Alex to knock on the door. She swallowed nervously when he did not appear. He is probably going to jump at my window and make me scream, she told herself. Alex could be so juvenile sometimes.

But Alex still did not appear.

Natalie was steeling herself to get out of the car to look for her boyfriend when she saw flashing red and blue lights approaching along the road. Relief flooded her, making her light-headed. Thank God, the police had come. She and Alex would probably get in trouble for parking, but Natalie didn't care. She just wanted to find Alex and go home.

Suddenly, the police car slammed on its brakes and two men leapt out. Then Alex's car shook as a thunderous wind rushed around it. Something scraped the roof over Natalie's head, and she could hear the police officers firing their guns. Natalie screamed as a huge dark shadow flew off into the night.

One of the officers ran to Alex's car and pounded on her door. Still screaming, Natalie unlocked it and threw herself into his arms. The officer hustled her toward the police car as something unearthly screamed above them. Natalie ducked instinctively as the horrible flapping creature dive-bombed them. The police officer pushed Natalie to the ground and shielded her with his body. The monster's claws ripped his back to shreds right through his bulletproof vest. Natalie heard the second officer fire two more shots. Then she heard the monster fly away over the trees.

Tears and mud coursed down Natalie's face as the wounded officer pulled her up and helped her into the patrol car. "My date," she cried suddenly. "Alex was outside with that . . . that thing! What happened to Alex?"

The officers looked grave and shook their heads. "Don't look, miss," the first officer said. But Natalie couldn't help herself. She glanced at the parked vehicle, illuminated by the flashing lights of the patrol car, and saw massive claw marks etched into the hood. A small bundle huddled on top of the rain-soaked roof. For a moment, Natalie's eyes refused to understand what they were seeing. Then the officer touched the bundle, and Alex's head fell toward the headlights, blue eyes staring blankly at nothing, face twisted in a rictus of fear. His chest was gaping open, and his half-chewed heart lay on the muddy ground at the officer's feet.

21

The Witch's Shoulder

WISE COUNTY, VA

One day, out of the clear blue, my sheep started dropping dead in the field. I'm a shepherd, so I've seen sheep pass in my time. But these sheep were bursting with health afore they up and died. One minute they'd be butting heads or gamboling playfully; the next moment they were flat on the ground—dead as a doornail.

"I just don't understand it," I said to my wife the night a fifth sheep keeled over in the middle of the field. "There ain't nothing wrong with them. I had the sheep doc in to check the lot of them. He even opened up one of the dead ones to have a look. They are fine. So why are they dropping like flies?"

My wife shook her head. "If you ask me, I'd say they were bewitched. Maybe you'd better talk to the conjure woman that lives over on the plantation and see what she says."

I hadn't thought of asking the conjure woman. But the doc hadn't helped at all, *and* he'd charged me a big fee to boot. I didn't have anything to lose by consulting the conjure woman, so I hied over to the plantation come sundown and asked around until I found the conjure lady cooking over the fire in a cabin packed with young 'uns. As soon as she saw me, she sent

THE WITCH'S SHOULDER

them young 'uns up to the loft to play and sat me down with a cup of tea.

"What's the problem?" she asked. She had a sweet, sympathetic face, and my troubles just poured out of me at the sight of her compassionate dark eyes. I told her about my sheep dying and the doc charging me to do nothing and my fear that I'd lose the whole flock. She listened intently and then asked me to describe each death in detail. When I finished, she gave a deep sigh and sat back in her chair.

"Honey, you done got you a bad curse on that flock of yours."

"That's what my wife said," I agreed with a sigh.

"I'm gonna tell you how to break this curse. And you best follow my instructions to the letter, or more of your sheep are gonna die."

When I solemnly promised to follow her instructions to the letter, she told me what to do. And she made me repeat it back to her to be sure I got it right. Then she gave me some biscuits to take home to my wife and shooed me out of the cabin afore her young 'uns—who were making a hullabaloo—came crashing down through the ceiling.

My wife came a-running out the front door when she saw me coming up the lane with my lantern.

"What did the conjure woman say?" she gasped.

"You were right. Them sheep are cursed," I said and told her everything the conjure woman had told me.

I got up early the next morning, determined to follow the conjure woman's instructions to the letter. I went to the barn where I'd placed the fifth dead sheep and carefully carved out the shoulder. Then I went into the kitchen, where my wife had reduced the fire in the stove to a bunch of warm coals. Very carefully we put the shoulder in the oven to bake. The conjure woman had told us to warm it up real slow before baking it for the best results. And she told us that if anyone came to our house, we weren't to let them borrow or steal anything from the house, and on no account were we to give them anything to eat or drink. It sounded a bit strange, but I'd promised to obey her instructions, and that's what I was gonna do.

It took two hours for that sheep shoulder to warm up to the point where it was ready for baking. Nobody had stopped by up to that point, and I'd just about decided nobody was gonna when my wife hurried to the window, crying "Look!"

Our neighbor's wife was hurrying up the lane toward us, though it was too early for a sociable call. She knocked on the door, and we let her in, watching her closely. She wanted to borrow some meal, but we told her we were out of meal. Then she asked for a drink of water, but my quick-witted wife told her that we'd drunk the last of the water from the well and had to go back for more. Then she hustled the neighbor-woman out the door so fast she didn't have time to steal anything from the house.

Our behavior must have seemed strange, but we weren't taking any chances. The conjure lady had said that anyone might be the witch.

A quarter hour later, the fellow who assisted me in the sheep field arrived. I sent him off with the flock without letting him inside the house. I hoped he wasn't the witch, but appearances could be deceiving, as the conjure lady had been quick to tell me. Even the minister came by to drop off some pamphlets for my wife to distribute at the Ladies Aid meeting, which she was having at our house the next day but one.

"Surely the minister isn't a witch," my wife exclaimed when she saw him riding his horse up the lane. But I made her go outside to greet him, and she took the pamphlets before he could dismount from his horse. All the while, inside the house the smell of roasting sheep shoulder was gradually filling the downstairs.

As my wife waved the minister off down the lane, the neighbor-woman came hurrying up, looking even more agitated than before. She met my wife in the yard and begged her for some salt.

"I'm afraid we ain't got no salt," I said from the doorway.

"No salt! Surely you do. Let me look," said the neighbor-woman, and she barged right past me into the house. My wife and I followed her quickly, exchanging alarmed glances.

"No salt," my wife said firmly, blocking the pantry door with her body.

The neighbor-woman twitched and turned to glare at our oven, where the shoulder was slowly getting hot. "I'm thirsty," she said fretfully. "Did you get the water from the well yet?"

"We've been a tad busy this morning," I said, firmly shoving her toward the door. "I ain't had time."

The neighbor-woman slipped past me again and tried to knock open the oven door.

"What are you roasting in there?" she asked. I blocked the oven door with my shepherd's crook before she could get it open.

"So nice of you to call," my wife said then, stepping in front of the neighbor-woman and taking her firmly by the arm. (Was it me, or did the neighbor woman wince when my wife jostled her shoulder?) A moment later the neighbor-woman was walking down the lane, with frequent looks back over her shoulder.

"Could it be her?" I asked my wife as soon as our neighbor disappeared from view. "She's acting awful strange."

"I bet it is her," my wife replied. "Remember last month when her husband wanted to buy our property with the stream running through it to pasture his cows? And you said no because we needed it for our sheep. I bet this is his wife's revenge against us for refusing to sell."

"You could be right," I said thoughtfully. The husband hadn't seemed too bothered by my refusal, but his wife had taken it as a personal insult.

My wife added a few more sticks to the fire as we spoke, and the sheep shoulder started to sizzle inside the oven. It was turning a nice brown color when we heard running footsteps coming down the lane. Afore I reached the front door, the neighbor-woman burst inside. "For God's sake, get the shoulder off the fire! Get it off quick! You're killing me!" She tore off the sleeve covering her left shoulder with shaking fingers. Underneath her dress, the woman's shoulder was the same deep shade of brown as the roasting shoulder of mutton, and I could hear it sizzling.

"Are you done cursing my sheep?" I asked sternly.

"I'm done! I'm done. Take it off the fire," she begged.

"Swear to it," my wife said, equally stern, and made her repeat the magic words the conjure lady had taught us. They were just gibberish to us, but they meant something to the neighbor-woman. She turned real pale, and I could tell she didn't want to say them. But her shoulder was burning up before our eyes, and she had no choice. When she uttered the last word, a mighty thunderclap came right out of a clear-blue sky; the neighbor-woman fell to her knees sobbing.

That's that, I thought, and I took the mutton off the fire. The neighbor-woman gasped with relief, and my wife gave her a wet cloth and some soothing ointment to put on her burned shoulder before sternly sending her away.

"Should we tell her husband she's a witch?" I asked my wife when the woman was gone.

"No need," my wife replied. "If he doesn't already know, he'll figure it out when he sees her shoulder. Besides," she added thoughtfully, "I think them magic words the conjure woman gave us may have taken her witchcraft away from her. They were that strong!"

Remembering the thunderclap, I had to agree.

That evening I went to the conjure lady's house with a big basket of vegetables and fruit from my garden and a lamb from my flock. I told her the whole story, and a grin spread all over her beautiful round face.

"Honey, she won't never bother you again," the conjure lady promised.

And she never did.

22

The Cursed Quilt

Bertha was not my favorite relative. She was bold as brass, with a sharp tongue and a bullying manner that did not endear her to me. Worse, she turned coy and sweet around boys and adults, hiding her true colors behind a false front. So when she moved in with my family after her folks passed, I was not pleased. Bertha was older than the rest of us, and she bossed us around something cruel. Mama saw through her conniving, but Papa was completely taken in.

All us girls shared a room, and Bertha and I had to sleep in the same bed. I ended up with twelve inches of space and Bertha took the rest. Anytime I tried to claim more territory, she'd kick me until I moved, pretending all the while that she was fast asleep.

As soon as I was old enough, I got work in the local mercantile. The owners offered to provide room and board as well as my wage, so I stayed in town during the week and went home for Sunday dinner. It was a relief to get away from Bertha, but I couldn't figure out why she didn't take the job herself. It was a fine opportunity for a girl from a poor family, but Bertha let the position go to me. I figured she preferred bossing the

THE CURSED QUILT

young 'uns over doing an honest day's work. But it turned out she had something else in mind.

Folks shopping at the mercantile started gossiping about Bertha and the preacher's boy. He'd been going with a girl named Bess for nearly a year, but dropped her as soon as Bertha looked his way. Lord almighty, I was furious. Bess was a nice girl and didn't deserve to be thrown over for someone like Bertha.

I heard that Bess was heartbroken and had pleaded with Bertha to let the preacher's son go. Bertha, of course, had refused. There was some speculation that Bess might be in the family way, so devastated was she by the whole situation.

Before a month had passed, Bertha and the preacher's boy were engaged to wed. Her future papa-in-law looked embarrassed when he made the announcement on Sunday. Bess started crying softly into her handkerchief and her Mama took her away. Her Granny, who was the town herbalist and healer, sat stiff and disapproving in the pew, glaring at the preacher and his son. But she turned all soft and sweet when she met Bertha in the churchyard after the sermon.

"Congratulations to ye," she said, taking Bertha's hand into her gnarled grip. "I'm making ye a quilt for yer new household."

Bertha smirked and tossed her blond curls. "That is right kind of you, Granny," she said and winked at me over the old lady's shoulder.

Two weeks later, Granny brought a pink and green quilt to church and presented it to Bertha. "The pattern's called Catch My Breath," Granny told Bertha. "It's a wedding quilt, so you must sleep under it every night to dream of your true love. And it will add spice to the marriage bed, if'n you know what I mean."

Bertha cooed over the quilt and showed it to everyone, including Bess. When we got home after church, she went right to our room and tucked it carefully on her side of the bed. It was a lovely quilt, all soft greens and pinks. I'd never seen the pattern before. It was full of circles and oblongs made out of many small triangles. If you looked at it just right, it looked like a menacing face with an open mouth full of sharp teeth. There was a faint smell of herbs coming from the quilt. I smelled tansy, rue, mugwort, and pennyroyal. Those were strange herbs to give to a bride. I shivered suddenly.

"I've never heard of a Catch My Breath quilt," I said. "I still don't understand why Bess's grandmother would give you a wedding quilt."

"She probably invented the pattern just for me," Bertha said smugly, tossing her curls. "And she gave me the quilt so everyone would know I am a much better match for the preacher's son than silly old Bess."

She walked away with her nose in the air. I sighed and went down to help Mama with the Sunday dinner.

I was shocked when I saw Bertha at church the next week. She was pale and there were dark rings under her eyes. Her perky blonde curls were drooping and there were lines around her lips.

"What's wrong with Bertha?" I whispered to Mama during the first hymn.

"She ain't sleeping too good," Mama told me. "Hush now. We'll talk after dinner."

Bertha was her usual bossy self in the churchyard, but I couldn't help noticing that she walked kind of stiff on the way back to the cove.

"She's been having nightmares," Mama told me after dinner as we washed up the dishes. "Says a dark figure drifts into her room and leans on her chest each night. She wakes up screaming and gasping for breath."

"You don't reckon . . . " I paused, wondering how much to say. Mama raised an eyebrow at me. "You don't reckon it's that Catch My Breath quilt Granny gave her, bringing on the dreams?"

"Pshaw, it ain't nothing of the sort. It's bridal nerves, I expect," Mama said. "The wedding's only a few weeks away and there's so much to do to get ready to set up housekeeping. I don't know how we are going to be ready in time."

Mama was right about all the work. Every minute I wasn't at the mercantile, I was sewing napkins for Bertha's hope chest or making lace or running errands. It was a real whirlwind of activity. Bertha didn't seem to be doing much of the work herself, except standing for fittings for her fancy wedding dress. She seemed paler each time I saw her. The lines on her face grew more pronounced and she held herself at a funny angle as if her back hurt her. Mama said she still had nightmares about a dark figure pressing the air out of her chest. A couple of times, Mama found Bertha with her head all wrapped up in the quilt. "It's no wonder she feels like she can't breathe," Mama scolded. "I keep telling her to tuck it in before she goes to sleep at night. But half the time she doesn't remember."

"I think you should take that quilt away from her, Mama," I said. "I think it's cursed."

But Mama didn't believe in curses. And Bertha was so proud of that quilt that she wouldn't listen to me when I told her that I thought the quilt was causing the dreams. "You're just jealous.

And you're right to be. I'm getting married and you'll be an old maid," she jeered.

The wedding day arrived, and we helped Bertha do her hair up nice. The fancy dress looked real fine, but Bertha wasn't at her best. She was too thin, there was no color in her face, and her curls had lost their bounce. But she was as coy and bossy as ever, and the look of dawning terror on the preacher boy's face when she marched down the aisle and took his arm told me he'd finally realized what he was getting into.

During the wedding supper, I sought out Granny. "Where is Bess?" I asked her. "I haven't seen her in town."

"Bess is staying with her cousin," Granny said. "There's a nice farmer in that village who would make a good husband." And father. Neither of us said it, but we both understood.

I reached into my pocket and pulled out a lace-edged handkerchief that I'd made while I was doing all the extra sewing for Bertha's wedding.

"It's a gift for Bess. I hope everything comes right for her," I said, handing it to Granny.

"I'll be sure she gets it," Granny said. "Thank ye."

We gave Bertha and her new husband a rousing send-off. They were staying in a remote hunting cabin for their honeymoon, before returning to set up housekeeping in a small house behind the preacher's place. Bertha took the new quilt with her, since Granny had hinted it would make the marriage bed even sweeter.

No one heard anything from the happy couple for several days. We figured they'd decided to extend their honeymoon, so no one was worried, though more than one ribald remark was made.

After a week, the preacher and Papa decided enough was enough. The couple must be getting low on food, and you couldn't live on nothing but love and air. They went to the hunting cabin to visit the newlyweds and ask them to come home. When they stepped inside, they found Bertha and the preacher's boy dead on the bed, the wedding quilt wrapped tightly around their throats.

23

The New Mill

It just so happened that Jack was down on his luck. He'd run out of money and so he took to wandering about, looking for work. That's how he found himself in this here valley. Now one little village hereabouts had never prospered from the time it was first settled. It was rumored that a secret coven of witches lived nearby and made life a misery for anyone who crossed them. Cows went dry. Pigs dropped dead in their pens. Chickens wouldn't lay. Things round here were a right mess.

Now Jack heard tell of a mill owner who was having more trouble than most. His new mill was said to be cursed and nobody would hire on with him. The owner was willing to pay top dollar to anyone brave enough to take on his cursed mill. So Jack headed to the owner's house and said to him: "I hear you need some help."

"Yessir, I do," the miller said. "I've got me a new mill, but its cursed. Every durned feller I've hired to run it was killed on his first night. Something poisoned 'em. If I can't lift the curse on the place, I'll lose all my money."

"I ain't skeered of no curse," Jack boasted. "Take me down there and I'll run your mill for you."

THE NEW MILL

The two men walked down to the site of the new mill and looked the place over. The mill was done up real nice and the equipment was in good order. The owner had even fixed up an old log house with a fireplace, so the miller had a place to eat and sleep. The only strange thing about the log cabin was twelve little windows high up on the walls that didn't bring in much light.

"I'll take the job," Jack said. "And I won't get poisoned tonight neither."

"Suit yourself. It's your funeral," the owner of the mill said. "I'll give you half the wages up front, and some rations for your supper tonight. You can start right away."

Word spread like wildfire through the cove. Folks were so glad the new mill was running that they lined up to get their corn ground. Jack was kept busy from sunup to sundown. He was plumb tuckered by the time the last person paid for their grinding and headed home.

Jack had just shut down the equipment and turned the water out of the mill race when along came a one-eyed feller with a long gray beard, riding an ornery mule. Jack sighed when he saw the sack of corn on the feller's back, but he walked over to greet 'im.

"How-do, Jack," the old feller said.

Jack was surprised. "How'd you know my name?" he asked. "I ain't never seen you before."

"I'm a stranger to you," said the old feller. "But I know many things, Jack. Now I've come a long way and I wonder if'n you could grind some corn for me. I know it's passed quittin' time, but I couldn't get here sooner."

"Sure, I'll help you out," Jack said. "Wait here for a-piece while I get the mill started and then I'll do you right."

Jack turned on the waterwheel and ground up the man's corn for him. When he carried the heavy sack of meal back to the mule, the old feller said: "Jack, you is the first one that done right by me at this new mill. I've got a reward fer ya."

"T'aint necessary, sir," Jack said politely. "Hit was my pleasure."

But the old feller insisted. He pulled a silver knife out of his ragged coat pocket and handed it to Jack. "Hit's good against witches," he told Jack.

The knife was a real work of art. Jack admired it and thanked the old feller. Then he helped settle the sack of corn meal on the mule and watched him ride away into the dark.

Jack put the silver knife into his pocket and walked to the log cabin to build up a fire and fix him some supper. The moon was rising, and it shone in the twelve small windows, making the inside of that log cabin bright as day.

Jack was cutting up his ration of meat with the silver knife when suddenly the whole room went dark. If it weren't for the fire in the hearth, Jack couldn't have seen anything at all. He looked up in surprise, thinkin' a cloud had come over the moon. But it wasn't a cloud. There were twelve black cats setting in them twelve windows. Every last one of them was staring at Jack with shining eyes.

Jack was real surprised. He probably should have been skeered half to death, but he was a brave feller. He wasn't going to run away from a good job on account of some creepy black cats. He shrugged it off and went back to slicing meat. Why should he care if twelve black cats wanted to keep 'im company?

Jack put the meat into the skillet and started cooking it over the fire. Gravy filled up the bottom of the pan and the meat sizzled. It smelled s'good Jack's stomach took to growling. One by one, he turned the strips of meat with his silver knife so they cooked nice and even.

Jack had most forgot about them black cats, until he heard one of them jump down from its window. When he looked up from the skillet, a black cat near as big as a 'coon was setting right next to him. It stretched its paw toward the skillet, meowing: "Sooop dollll."

The words sent a shiver down Jack's spine. They sounded like a black magic spell. He knew sop meant to soak something in gravy. And "doll" was the word his old granny used for a person's soul. He realized this black cat had come here to poison the gravy in his pan so it could kill him dead and take away his soul.

Jack jerked the skillet out of reach and glared at the black cat. He wasn't going to be poisoned by some foul magic critter like them other fellers what worked the mill. "Keep yer durned paw away from my meat," he said, shaking the silver knife at the black cat. "You sop in my skillet and I'll cut yer paw off."

The black cat's glowing eyes narrowed in rage. It drew back and glared at Jack. The eleven black cats behind it stirred on their windowsills. Jack ignored them all and kept cooking his food.

"Sooop dollll," the cat mewled again. It reached for the skillet with a huge paw. Jack jerked the pan away and pointed the silver knife at the creature. It bared its long teeth at him. "I told you not to sop yer paw in my meat. You try it again; I'll take it off."

The cat hissed at him. Jack gave it a vicious smile, baring all his teeth. It was Jack against the cat, and he planned to win this fight. The black cat switched its long tail and its eleven followers hissed in unison. Jack ignored them all. He put some meal and seasonings into the pan and stirred everything around until he had a thick gravy. His meal was ready to eat.

Suddenly, the big ol' black cat sprang forward and sopped its foot in Jack's gravy. "Sooop dollll," it howled in triumph.

Skeered for his soul, Jack slashed down with his knife and cut the black cat's paw off. The foot tumbled into the skillet. The black cat screamed and leapt toward the open window. The other cats yowled in panic and every last one of 'em vanished before Jack could turn himself around.

"You done ruined my dinner," Jack shouted after them. He threw the tainted meat and gravy into the fire. When the black cat's paw hit the flames, it turned into a woman's hand.

"Gosh almighty," Jack swore, knocking the hand from the fire. There was a fancy wedding ring on one finger. He wondered who it belonged to. Jack wrapped the severed hand in paper and put it in a safe spot. Then he scoured his skillet real good to get the poison out before he cooked up another portion of meat for his supper. He didn't think the black cats would return.

In the morning, Jack heard the owner calling to him from the mill yard.

"I figured you was dead," the owner said when Jack came out to meet him. "I'm sure glad to be wrong."

"They tried, but I'm a hard feller to kill," Jack said, and told the owner the whole story.

When Jack showed him the woman's hand with the ring, the mill owner liked to faint. "That's my wife's hand," he gasped. "I gave 'er that ring nearly twenty years ago."

Jack felt terrible for the mill owner. There was only one kind of person what could change themselves into a black cat. And that was a witch.

"I knew she was a-going out sometimes at night to meet with some ladies in the valley. But I never imagined they was the coven of witches what was plaguing our village," the mill owner said. "My wife was ailing this morning and didn't get out of bed. It must be on account of her severed hand. She asked me to send for her friends to give 'er some comfort. They're probably meetin' at my place right now."

Jack and the owner walked to the house to check on the witches. Sure enough, the members of the coven were all there meeting with their ailing leader. The miller sent Jack back to work at the mill and then he went inside with the severed hand to talk to his wife.

About an hour later, a young 'un came running down from the cove, shouting for everyone standing in line at the mill to come quick. The mill owner's house was on fire. By the time they reached the house, it was too late. The fire was burning so hot and so fast no one could put it out. It burned up all twelve witches and the mill owner too. Jack figured that the owner must have set the fire himself to kill off that coven of witches, and probably stayed with them as penance since it wasn't right for him to kill his own wife.

Once the witches were gone, folks in the cove finally started prospering. As for Jack? I heard he got himself a pretty wife and is still working that mill. Makes a good living and has a passel of young 'uns to pass it on to. So, everything turned out just fine.

Spear-Finger

"Uwe la na tsiku. Su sa sai."

The medicine man was meditating before the fire when the sweet voice drifted down to him from the mountaintop. He shivered, for there was a menace within the voice, in spite of the loveliness of its intonation.

The voice came again: "Uwe la na tsiku. Su sa sai."

His mind automatically translated the words: "I eat liver, yum, yum." The medicine man's blood ran cold, for he knew then that he was hearing the voice of the Spear-Finger singing to herself as she made her way toward their village.

At that moment, the voice was drowned by a gust of wind that bent the trees and rattled the bushes. A great flash of lightning ripped through the sky, making the night bright as noon. Thunder shook the whole valley.

The medicine man knew that Spear-Finger was marching down from on high, throwing massive stones between each mountain peak and using them as bridges. Every step she took made the earth shudder and rocks crack. He knew if he hiked to the peak in the morning, he would see footprints sunk deep into the earth under the weight of her stone body. The medicine

SPEAR-FINGER

man hurriedly doused his fire and ran back to the village to warn his chief.

The morning after the storm, runners were dispatched to warn the other villages that Spear-Finger had come to their mountains with her disregard for human life and her taste for liver. Even now, she lurked along the dark pathways and traversed the streambeds, perching in hidden crags and observing the patterns of the people in this new place. She would feed on anyone who strayed too close to her hiding place.

Spear-Finger's body was encased in a stone skin so that no spear could penetrate her flesh, and the forefinger of her right hand was made of a long thin stone that was sharp as a knife and could slice a person open with one flick. And Spear-Finger was a shapeshifter who could take on the guise of a helpless old woman, a young succulent deer, or a craggy warrior.

The men started hunting in groups, and their wives took care to bring their children into their lodges each night. Fear trembled in every heart, for who could protect them if Spear-Finger came to their village? "Stay in the lodge," mothers warned their little ones. "Do not walk alone in the woods, for Spear-Finger is near!"

At first, the children shivered and obeyed. But as the weeks passed with no sign of the monster, the children ceased their vigilance and started playing in the fields outside their village. And so they were unprepared when a sweet old grandmother came hobbling down the path toward them. "Come, my children," she said to them in a gentle voice, "Come let Grandmother brush your hair. It has grown tangled in your games, and your parents will be displeased."

The small daughter of the chief ran to the old lady and sat in her lap. She loved to have her hair combed and submitted to the woman's touch, as the grandmother sang softly: "Uwe la na tsiku. Su sa sai." The child only shuddered a little when the stone finger stabbed through her skin and cut her liver out with a single twist.

When Spear-Finger set the child back on her feet and bade her walk home, the whole world swam oddly before the child's eyes. The little girl took a few steps before falling over dead. By the time she dropped to the ground, Spear-Finger was gone.

The other children had quite forgotten the friendly grandmother who had passed through their field until they found their playmate lying dead. Then they screamed, and the mothers and old men came running, along with a few warriors returned early from their hunt. The little girl was carried with many wails into the village, and the chief and his wife wept in despair.

Back in the woods, Spear-Finger changed shape, disguising herself as a warrior whom she had killed early that morning while he was out hunting. The warrior's wife was completely fooled by the disguise. She left Spear-Finger alone in the lodge that night while she tended the birth of her sister's first child. The monster made short work of the little ones left in her care. By the time the wife returned, her children were dead, their livers gone.

Reeling backward at the gruesome sight, the wife screamed in terror as her neighbors came running to see what was wrong. But there was nothing they could do to comfort her. Spear-Finger had cut her way out of the back of the lodge and disappeared. They found her husband's dead body beside the river and buried him with his children.

From that moment, every person entering the village was suspect—for if the monster could fool the wife of a warrior, who else might she fool? The medicine man was busy day and night performing the magic to confirm all the villagers going about their daily tasks were not Spear-Finger in disguise. Men eyed their wives in suspicion and kept weapons close at hand, and wives refused to leave the children alone with their fathers.

The next morning, two men were sent to set fire to the underbrush in the local grove so the tribe would have easy access to the trees during the harvest. It was a short task that should have taken a single morning. Yet hour after hour passed, and there was no sign of the men's return. Finally, a group was sent to look for them. The bodies of the men were found a few hundred yards into the grove with their hearts crushed and their livers removed. Word of the murder spread like wildfire through the village. Panicking people raced to the lodge of their chief to demand protection from the monster.

Frightened and enraged by the monster who had killed his only child and terrorized his village, the chief called a council of all the surrounding villages and demanded a solution. How could they rid themselves of the Spear-Finger? Many ideas were discussed and discarded before the medicine man proposed that they dig a pit and trap the creature inside. Perhaps then they might examine her close at hand and discover if there was a fatal weakness beneath her skin of stone. No one had a better solution, and so they decided to follow the medicine man's plan.

Under cover of darkness, a large pit was dug on the path outside the village. The next morning, the warriors gathered on either side of the path, hidden among the brush, and a fire was set once again in the chestnut grove. Lured by the cover of the smoke and the promise of fresh liver, Spear-Finger came down from the mountain at speed, hoping to surprise the warriors burning the brush as she had done previously. She slowed when she reached the path to the village and took on her usual disguise of an old woman, hoping to ease the fears of her victims.

As she came hobbling toward the village through the smoke, the warriors gazed at one another in bewilderment. Surely this harmless-looking old woman could not be the fierce monster they had come to trap. But the medicine man gave them a signal: Wait and watch.

The old woman gave a sharp cry of surprise when she stepped onto the brush covering the pit and plummeted to the bottom. Her cry turned into an ear-shattering howl of rage as Spear-Finger realized she had been tricked.

The warriors sprang out from both sides of the path and surrounded the pit, arrows knocked. Below them, a stone-skinned monstrosity with foul locks and a withered brown face leapt about the pit, roaring in anger. Then she reached her sharp stone finger right into the dirt and flicked out a huge rock, which she tossed onto the floor of the pit, followed swiftly by another and then another. She was going to build her way out of the pit! The chief gave the order to fire, and the warriors shot their arrows again and again at the creature, but they bounced uselessly off her stone skin.

Spear-Finger ignored the encircling humans and brushed occasionally at the arrows as if they were no more than bothersome gnats. She kept pulling out stones and piling them into a ramp.

"Poles, spears!" the chief cried when it became obvious that the creature would soon be high enough to climb out of the pit.

Several tribesmen ran into the grove and hacked down long branches to use as poles, while others fetched their spears. They thrust at the Spear-Finger, harrying her and pushing her off the ramp again and again. She gnashed her sharp brown teeth at them and parried their blows with her sharp stone finger, cutting off a few spear tips and nearly decapitating a warrior who leaned too close.

"Pray," the chief ordered his medicine man. "Pray to all the gods for help. If this monster gets out of the pit, we are all dead!"

The medicine man began chanting a prayer, begging the gods to save them from the monster with her stone finger and her lust for blood.

At that moment, a tiny titmouse, still radiant with the glow of heaven, came flying into the midst of the mighty battle, crying "Un un un," the closest it could come to saying "u'na hu," which means heart.

The medicine man gasped: "The heart! Aim for the monster's heart!"

Immediately the warriors notched their arrows and shot the creature in the chest again and again, while others pummeled her with their spears. Spear-Finger laughed at them and climbed farther up the ramp, taking a swipe at a warrior with her sharp finger and cutting off his hand.

The warrior fell to the ground and crawled away in an agony of pain. Seeing the glowing titmouse in the brush beside the path, he grabbed it, crying: "Lying creature! See what your lies have caused!" And he cut out part of its tongue. But the titmouse struggled and pecked until he let it go, whereupon it returned to the heavens with only half of its tongue.

"Peace, my brother," said the medicine man as he tended the wound. "The titmouse was right. We must find the creature's heart to kill it. It just didn't know how to tell us where its heart is."

As he spoke, a lovely, glowing chickadee swept down from the heavens and perched for a moment on Spear-Finger's hand, beside the stone finger she used as a knife.

"There," the medicine man cried, understanding the second bird's message. "Aim for the hand! The heart is in the hand!"

Spear-Finger gave a horrible cry when she heard the medicine man's words. She took a swipe at the chickadee, which flew gracefully away. For a moment her palm was exposed, and the men could plainly see the pulsing heart in its center. The chief took aim and sent an arrow right through the creature's heart in memory of his daughter.

Spear-Finger wailed horrifically as she landed among the broken spears and arrows at the bottom of the pit. She twitched several times and then died, her stone finger still waving above her grotesque form. All at once, the monster's dead body turned into a hazy, foul-smelling smoke that whirled around and around before exploding upward, high into the sky, where it disbursed in the wind. And that was the end of Spear-Finger.

25

Boojum

When I was a young man, I worked as a carpenter, and I made a pretty penny doing it. I married early and already had a couple of young 'uns when I was asked to do a piece of work in Chattanooga, building up a fancy house for a rich feller and his wife who took a notion to move there. It was too far to go home each night, so I stayed in an old cabin they had on the property and drove home on the weekends to see my family.

Now I'd bought a secondhand Model T Ford, the very first car owned by anyone in the family, and I was right proud of it. Kept it polished up good and was careful to keep it away from overhanging trees and bushes that might scratch up my paint. I was as protective of that car as a broody hen with her chicks, so I drove her slow and careful up the twists and turns of the mountain and then back down the other side whenever I went home on the weekend; careful to avoid any potholes. I didn't want a blown-out tire up there on the mountain. There was a twenty-mile stretch with no houses on it, and I didn't fancy walking out that far and back for a part if I broke my car on a bump.

BOOJUM

Late one afternoon when the new house was more than halfway done, I got called to the company phone. It was my wife, looking for me to come home quick cause our young 'uns were sick and she needed my help. It was already quittin' time, and twilight was closing in fast in the shadow of the mountains. I had a long drive ahead of me up that narrow, twisty road. I'd never driven it at night, so I felt real nervous. But "sooner started, sooner done," as my granny always said, so I gassed up my Model T and headed for home.

A soft summer breeze caressed my face as I drove up the mountain. The only sound was the whirl of my tires and the only things visible in my headlights were the laurel bushes on the side of the road and the canopy of trees above my head.

I had just reached the twenty-mile empty stretch when a strange, rotten smell drifted through the air. I wrinkled my nose as I rounded the bend and hit the brakes in alarm. Standing in a water ditch on the side of the road was a huge barrel-shaped figure with a hairy body, extremely long arms, and a flat brown face. Its eyes were round and dark, its ears were small, and its nose was flat. Its feet were huge, and I reckoned the man . . . person . . . critter . . . weighed several hundred pounds. I never seen anything like it, but I'd heard tell of an ape-critter called a Boojum or a Bigfoot, and I reckoned I was looking straight at one right now.

The Boojum squinted at me in the headlights, as if he was trying to figure out what kind of critter I was. It would have been funny, only my heart was pitty-patting so hard I couldn't laugh right then. After a minute of staring, that big hairy critter stalked up to me, leaned over the car and stepped on the running board. My mouth dropped open, which was a mistake because woo-ee did that Boojum smell; like stale sweat mixed with rotting garbage. I don't know the last time that hairy ape-man took a bath, but he was long overdue.

The Boojum reached way down with his hairy arms, which were twice as wide as mine, and opened the door with fingers that were a good ten inches long. He got into the passenger seat of my Model T, as cool as you please. He looked me over, and his big dark eyes had twin flames in them, reflecting the headlights. There wasn't anything I could do. If'n he wanted to, he could scoop me up one-handed and toss me down the mountain, he was that big.

"So mister, do you need a ride?" I asked in the polite tone my mama drilled into me as a young 'un. The Boojum didn't say nothing, just looked pointedly ahead, so I put my car back in gear and started driving carefully down that twisty dark road, avoiding the potholes and washboard sections whenever I could. I wasn't going to hurt my Model T for no one, not even a hairy Boojum hitchhiker that could have ate me for lunch and still had room for dessert.

I was so nervous; my hands were trembling on the steering wheel. But that old Boojum didn't say nothing to me. He just kept breathing heavily, each puff of air adding to the stench in the car. My nose just about stopped working with him so close. It was a good thing I had the windows down, or I might have suffocated.

To break the awkward silence, I told the Boojum about my wife's phone call and my sick young 'uns. I had two little ones already and a third on the way. Then I rambled on about my carpenter job down in Chattanooga and about how much it cost to keep up the Model T, and the little apple seedling that my wife was nurturing that came from my granny's prize-winning tree. Anything I could think of to pass the time.

We'd gone a good ten miles and I started wondering if the Boojum intended to come all the way home with me. I was trying to figure out how to explain my companion to Molly when the Boojum shifted suddenly in this seat, opened the car door, and stepped onto the running board. I obligingly stopped the Model T so he could get down and watched as the Boojum walked over to a barely discernable footpath on the side of the road.

"Have a good evening, sir," I called to him, and stepped on the gas. Getting out of there seemed like a good idea, right about then.

I glanced back when I came to the next bend. In the bit of moonlight that filtered through the trees branches overhead, I could see the tall hairy figure standing by the side of the road, watching me drive away. He looked a bit lonesome, to tell the truth. I wondered where he was going, and why it was so urgent that he'd hitched a ride in my Model T. With hairy legs that long, he probably could have gotten to his destination just as quickly walking as he did by riding in my car.

I rounded the bend and took a deep breath in relief. Which was a mistake, cause the car still smelled to high heaven of sweat and old garbage and well . . . of Boojum. I was shaking and sweating and babbling to myself the whole way home, overreacting to the strange situation. What a crazy adventure. No one would ever believe me. Folks thought the Boojum was just a story people told to entertain the young 'uns.

Molly came waddling out to the car to greet me, relief all over her pretty face. As soon as she caught a whiff of the

Boojum's scent, she reeled back and made a run for the bathroom. Carrying a young 'un made her sick to her stomach, and that Boojum smell was enough to make anyone lose their dinner.

I followed my wife into the house and went to the bedroom to check on the kids. They were asleep, but they stirred restlessly when they smelled their Boojum-scented Papa come in. I beat a hasty retreat before they woke and had me a good wash up before returning to the sickroom so Molly could get some rest.

"What in heaven's name was that smell?" she groaned as she curled up on our bed.

"I'll tell you all about it in the morning," I said, tucking her in with a scented sachet her granny had given us to help with stomach ailments.

It took a couple of days to get the young 'uns back on their feet so Molly was able to cope on her own. With things back to normal, I finally got a chance to wash the Model T to get rid of the Boojum scent. And don't you know, there were scratches all over the door handle where the Boojum's long fingernails gripped it! I showed them to Molly when I told her about my adventure.

"I don't mind picking up a needy hitchhiker," I exclaimed. "But darn it, that Boojum messed with my paint job! And just when I'd gotten the Model T polished up good. I'm going to charge him the next time he comes around wanting ride!"

Molly gave me a funny pursed-lip look that meant she was trying not to smile. "You do that, sweetheart," she said. "You charge that Boojum a dollar for every scratch. That will learn him!"

26

The Devil's Book

Back in the old days, before electric lights and such, a man named Gerald lived with his pretty wife, Mary Ann, on a small farm on the Kentucky side of the Gap. They were a happy couple, with two grown children, nice neighbors, and livestock enough to keep body and soul together.

One day Gerald went over to see his neighbor to ask for help mending a tricky place in his barn. When Gerald reached the neighbor's house, the wife came to the door and told Gerald that her husband was out in the fields. The wife invited Gerald inside to wait for her husband.

Gerald sat down and waited patiently while his neighbor's wife sat down at her wheel and started spinning some cotton into thread. She spun faster and faster until the whole floor was covered with thread. Gerald was amazed. Mary Ann couldn't spin thread like that. There must be some kind of trick to it, Gerald decided.

Wanting to get to the bottom of the mystery, Gerald asked his neighbor's wife if she would get him a drink. As soon as she went out the door with her bucket, he examined her spinning wheel. It looked the same as his wife's wheel. Then

THE DEVIL'S BOOK

Gerald looked underneath it. There was a small red rag under the spinning wheel. It looked like a piece of petticoat. Gerald clipped off a corner of the rag, put the wheel back exactly as the woman had left it, and sat down.

After drinking a dipper of water, Gerald told his neighbor's wife that he was going to try to find her man out in the fields. Wishing her good day, Gerald hurried out of the house. But instead of looking for his neighbor, Gerald went home to his wife.

"Mary Ann, I need you to do some spinning," he called as soon as he entered the house.

"But Gerald, I've finished the spinning for this year. We've already got more than enough yarn to fill the big loom twice over. And there's naught left of the wool saving this tiny pile. How in tarnation do you expect me to spin that?" Mary Ann asked, surprised by his request.

But Gerald insisted that Mary Ann spin the rest of her wool immediately.

Mary Ann knew her husband pretty well, and she knew he was up to something. But it was no use trying to figure it out when he was in this mood, so she got out her spinning wheel, loaded up the bobbin, adjusted the tension, and sat down with the small pile of leftover fleece in her lap.

"Before you start, Mary Ann, why don't I put this bit of red rag under your wheel?" said Gerald, taking the rag out of his pocket. Mary Ann looked at him suspiciously, but she let him place the red rag under her wheel and she began to spin.

To Mary Ann's astonishment, the wool seemed to leap through her hands, as if it could twist itself into thread without her help. The treadle under her foot seemed to be moving by itself, faster and faster. The wheel spun so quickly that the air around it started to sing. It was as if the wool and the wheel were making yarn without any help from her at all. The tiny pile of leftover wool on her lap should have been used up in a moment, but the pile never diminished. The bobbin filled up so rapidly it frightened her.

With a scream of fear, Mary Ann ripped her hands away from the wheel, jumped up, and shouted: "I don't know what devilment you're up to, Gerald, but I won't be a part of it." She ripped the thread off the bobbin, ran out the door, and dumped it in the deepest part of the creek.

Gerald grabbed up the bit of red rag and stuffed it in his pocket. He felt bad about scaring his wife, and decided he would apologize to her as soon as he finished his evening chores.

Gerald was heading back to the house after the milking was done when he came face-to-face with a large figure that looked something like a man, except it had a small pair of horns on its head. The sun seemed to glow red around the figure, which Gerald found mighty strange because the sun had already set behind the mountaintop. Gerald stopped dead and looked into the tall figure's burning black eyes. The figure bowed and held out a book to Gerald, saying, "Sign here, please."

"What do you mean, sign here? Sign for what? If you want me to sign that book, you've gotta hand it to me," Gerald snapped. He was mighty nervous of the glowing figure with the horns.

"I can't come over to you," the horned figure said.

Gerald saw that there was a glowing circle surrounding his body, which stopped a few inches from the horned figure. Gerald was frightened, but he reached over and took the book. When he opened it, he saw writing at the top of the first page: We and All We Possess Belong to The Devil. This was followed by the names of all his neighbors. At the top of the list was the name of the neighbor woman who had the red rag under her spinning wheel.

Gerald looked over at the horned figure. It was glaring at him with flaming eyes. Gerald was scared nearly to death, but he said, "I'm not signing this. I don't belong to the devil, and neither do my wife and children."

"That seems strange to me," said the horned figure, his eyes glowing brighter with each word. "You've been using witchcraft. What about that red rag you put under your wife's spinning wheel?"

Gerald felt the rag twitch in his pocket, then a pretty little red bird came flying out and landed on his wrist. The bird gave a horrible chuckle. It sounded like a demon—and so it was. It gave a second chuckle and flew over to perch on the shoulder of the horned figure.

Gerald knew he had to do something quickly. He turned the page over, wrote We and All We Possess Belong to The Lord, and signed his name to the page. Then he handed the book back.

The horned figure took one look at the book and gave a terrible, piercing scream before bursting into flames, smoke swirling around and around it. There was a bright flash and a smell of brimstone, and then Gerald fell onto the ground as the horned figure disappeared.

As soon as Gerald got back on his feet, he ran right to the house and told Mary Ann the whole story.

"We're not staying here," Gerald said. "I won't live in a place where all my neighbors have sold themselves to the devil."

Gerald and Mary Ann packed up and left the next day. Their children and their families also left after hearing Gerald's story.

There's no one living on that side of the hill anymore, just a few abandoned buildings and a burned spot where nothing will grow. Folks reckon that's the spot where the horned figure stood when it tried to get Gerald to sign its book. Everyone around these parts calls that spot "the devil's garden," and no one goes there.

27

The Murdered Miner

SPARTANBURG, SC

He was aching, tired, and covered in smelly mud when he saw the little house on the outskirts of town on a rainy evening in early spring 1827. He'd spent months searching for gold, and he was ready to abandon his search when he'd found placer gold in the foothills. He had a pretty darn good idea where to find the mother lode, but first he needed to stock up on supplies and buy better tools using the gold nuggets he found. The miner was heading toward the nearest town when the thunderstorm hit, frightening his mule so much the creature had bolted, throwing him off the wagon into the mud, where he'd lain in a daze, watching his wagon disappear into the distance. The fall had injured his head, and he staggered slowly down the road, hoping to find help somewhere.

When he saw lantern light in the window of the little house deep in the woods, he staggered in at the gate, hoping the occupants would have pity on him and take him in. He pounded on the door, and a moment later it opened and a middle-aged woman peered out cautiously. Behind her, a voice called: "Sister, who is it?"

THE MURDERED MINER

Before she could answer, the miner collapsed on the stoop, done in from his fall and subsequent long trek through the woods. The sisters clucked at each other and brought him inside. They tucked him into a blanket and when he awoke, they fed him soup and brought him warm water so that he could wash the mud off. They even found him some dry clothes left in the house by their deceased brother. The miner was grateful for the attention, and he didn't say no when they insisted he take a drink of their homemade remedy, which was mostly made up of moonshine.

It was the moonshine that did him in. Literally. He got roaring drunk and told the sisters all about the gold he discovered. He was still rambling when the younger sister hurried into the kitchen to take the kettle off the stove and returned with a sharp carving knife in her hand. He was shocked into silence when the knife was thrust into his heart. He stared at the handle in his chest for what seemed an eternity, and then fell over and died without another word. The sisters searched his dirty clothes and found a small pocketbook full of gold nuggets. They smiled at each other in satisfaction, and the elder sister went outside to dig a hole in the vegetable garden for their permanent guest.

A month passed while the sisters debated what to do with their newfound fortune. They couldn't spend it in town. People would talk. Finally, they decided they would walk to Spartanburg and hire a coach to take them north to Asheville, where their cousin—a notorious moonshiner—could advise them. Of course, he would make them split the gold with him, but it couldn't be helped.

The next afternoon, they tied on their bonnets and began the long walk toward town. It was a grim day with clouds so low they almost brushed the tops of the trees. The light was dim and uneven, and the sisters hurried along the road, hoping that a farmer might drive past and offer them a lift. An hour passed, and a light rain began to fall. The sisters were still alone on the road to town.

"Walk carefully, sister," said the elder. "This path will soon turn to mud."

"Carry your skirts higher, sister," advised the younger. "We don't want to look untidy when we get to town."

At that moment, they heard the jingle of a harness and the clip-clop of hooves behind them. The sisters turned, peering out from under their bonnets through the gray light. A wagon was coming toward them, pulled by a mule. It appeared to be full of digging and panning equipment, and the man driving the mule had the rough appearance of a miner. The sisters exchanged sly glances. Here was another lonely miner. They might get lucky twice. The elder sister glanced at her sister's handbag, which held the kitchen knife they always carried with them when they walked to town, for fear of robbers. The younger sister smiled and patted the handbag. Then she waved at the approaching wagon and drawled prettily: "Sir, can you give us a ride to town?"

The man on the wagon seat had a face that was mostly beard, just like the first miner. In fact, he resembled the first miner so much that the elder sister felt a pang in her chest. Surely this was not his brother, come searching for him? The miner stopped the wagon and beckoned for the sisters to join him. The younger sister sprang daintily aboard, and the elder sister pushed aside her misgivings and climbed up on the far side of the wagon.

The sisters sat on either side of the miner, and he continued his journey without a word spoken to either of them. The sisters politely said nothing about the stench rising off the miner, though they were both overwhelmed by it. *Really*, thought the elder, *he must not have bathed in months*. His clothes held the sickly-sweet smell of decay, as if he'd rolled in a compost heap and then perfumed himself with the meat of a long-dead deer. How vulgar. The elder sister put her handkerchief daintily to her nose and tried to breathe through it, to calm her roiling stomach.

On the far side of the driver, her younger sister gave a sigh as if she wanted to speak but couldn't. Glancing toward her, the elder sister's eye was caught by the gaunt cheekbones pushing through the man's skin. Really, the man could almost be a skeleton, he was so thin. And his bulging eyes stared straight ahead, like those of a dead fish. The elder sister shuddered and turned away.

The man's stench filled her nostrils and seemed to enter her bloodstream and move like poison through her whole body. The smell seemed to burn her under her skin. Then it turned to ice, and she shuddered in the seat. She wanted to get up and throw herself out of the wagon, but her body was heavy. So heavy.

The younger sister sighed again, as if in pain, and the elder sister glanced toward her. But the miner was still in the way, bulging eyes staring out at the misty rain without blinking. The skin of his face appeared grayer now, and—the elder sister swallowed suddenly—it looked gooier. It reminded her of the damp decay that curled along the edges of leaves of uneaten lettuce. *His skin was melting away*, she thought, burying her face in her handkerchief.

The man's stench no longer bothered her but his metamorphosis did. Once again, she tried to move her body, to jump off the wagon full of mining tools. But her legs felt brittle and frail, as if they could not hold her. As if her bones were rotting from the inside out. But how could bones rot? She glanced down at her long skirts, as if she might see through the thick covering to her agonized limbs. They were throbbing hot, cold, hot. So were her hands under the long gloves she wore. The elder sister pulled off a glove and gazed in horror at her hand. It was gray, and the skin looked gooey, as if it were rotting off her throbbing bones.

On the far side of the wagon, her sister sighed a third time. The elder turned in panic toward the sound, only to encounter the skeletal face of the miner, reduced now to a few ragged patches of skin with maggots writhing just behind the bones. The elder sister clapped her bare hand to her mouth, and felt the gray skin of her hand burn the flesh of her lips. She forced her eyes past the dead miner toward her sister and saw a skeleton wearing a bonnet tied under its jawbone. Bones peaked through her dainty walking dress, an hour before held so carefully above the mud by the gloved hand that was now tatters of damp cloth over withered gray skin and sharp splinters of finger bone. The skeleton turned toward the elder sister and said: "Sister, I do not feel well." Then it burst into flames, beginning with the too-clean hem of the walking dress and rapidly boiling upward with a smell of brimstone and sulfur. Moments later, the blackened bones of the skeleton rattled to the floor of the wagon.

The elder sister opened her mouth to scream, but there was nothing left to scream with. Her tongue and throat had rotted away. Her skin was melting off her bones in a gooey, smelly trickle. She smelled of rot and decay, and her eyes were beginning to burn from the inside out. She turned her head as her vision faded and stared at the miner driving the cart. A skeleton grinned back at her in triumph. Bony hands urged the glowing, translucent mule to walk faster as the elder sister's skirts began to burn.

28

The Goblin of Haint Hollow

GAINESVILLE, GA

Joe Cooper burst into my cabin without knocking; his small wiry body shaking in panic. "Hank! Hank! You got to help me," he panted, falling to his knees and clutching his chest over his thumping heart.

I jumped up from the wooden table that stood at the center of my one-room cabin, sending my stew bowl flying onto the floor.

"What's wrong, Joe? You look as if haints were after you!"

"They is, Hank! They is!" Joe staggered to his feet and fell into the chair beside the fireplace. He held trembling hands toward the blaze as my dog came wagging up to greet his old friend. "I was walking past Haint Hollow on my way to the mercantile to watch the checkers tournament, and I saw the goblin!"

"You dint!" I gasped, dabbing ruefully at my stew-covered overalls with the napkin tied around my neck.

"I did! It came racing across the road in the shape of a black cat," Joe said, his face going gray at the memory. "When it seen me, it hissed and started getting bigger. Next thing I knew, I was looking at a big ol' black panther with its fangs bared. I

THE GOBLIN OF HAINT HOLLOW

gave an almighty yell and hightailed it over here as fast as my legs would carry me. I ain't messin' with no black panther."

I stared at my buddy in alarm. Everybody knew there was a goblin in Haint Hollow. Folks said it dropped down from the trees and covered people's eyes with bony hands, putting terrible pictures into their minds and whispering darkly into their ears. Once it had them, the goblin wouldn't release its victims until dawn. A few folks in town blamed their premature white hair on the goblin, and it was said that one poor fellow hung himself in despair, unable to free his mind of the terrible images placed there by the goblin.

But Joe's story didn't gibe with other goblin-related tales. "You sure it was the goblin you seen?" I asked. "It dint act like the goblin, leastways, not according to the stories I heard."

"Listen, Hank. I dint stop to ask the haint what it was," Joe said in a wobbly voice. "I just run here as fast as I could."

Seein' that Joe was too upset to talk, I got him a mug of moonshine and poured myself another while I was at it. But my mind kept fussing with the problem. If Joe hadn't seen the goblin, then what had he seen? A black cat that transformed into a black panther sounded like a witch-woman to me. But why would a powerful witch-woman be scared of Joe? I looked over at my small friend. He was a skinny fellow with thinning brown hair and huge spectacles. He looked as if a heavy wind might blow him away.

"I'll drive you home in the wagon," I said when Joe finished his moonshine. "Your missus will be worrying."

"Mattie begged me not to walk to town tonight," Joe said, rising reluctantly from his seat by the fire. "She had a premonition that something horrible would happen to me if I went to town. Lord help me, I didn't believe her. I figured all the stories about the goblin were jest nonsense. But I tell you, Hank, that haint I seen tonight was real!" Joe started shaking all over again just thinking about it.

I hitched my horse, Old Nellie, to my wagon and we set off down the road toward Joe's place. I led the talk around to the checkers competition at the mercantile. Checkers ain't a game fer sissies, not the way we play. There was some heavy betting going on. The two top contenders were the blacksmith and the preacher. Tonight was part two of a three-part championship. I couldn't blame Joe for wanting to watch.

We were debating the merits of the two finalists as we entered Haint Hollow. While Joe talked, I kept my eyes on the trees overhanging the dark road. The air in the hollow was almighty cold for August. There was a light wind rustling the oak leaves overhead, and a crescent moon was playing hide-and-seek with some wispy gray clouds. I wasn't feeling too good about this journey.

Two things happened simultaneously. Old Nellie shied in her traces, and a dark figure swooped down into the wagon and clamped one huge skeletal hand over my eyes and the other over Joe's. "Gotcha!" hissed a sinister voice. The touch of that hand was an abomination. My skin crawled with loathing as fiery images of destruction and despair appeared in my mind.

Then I heard the piercing screech of a large cat coming from the back of the wagon. The loathsome hand fell abruptly from my eyes, and I whirled and kicked out at the twisted obscenity crouching behind my seat. My kick sent the creature sprawling at the feet of a black cat standing in the bed of the wagon. I glanced at Joe to see if he was all right. My wiry friend gaped at the scene through goblin-smeared glasses and shouted: "That's the haint I saw earlier!"

The black cat and the goblin stared fixedly at each another. As I watched, the skin of the haint swirled with grayish smoke, and the cat enlarged abruptly, becoming a massive black panther. It lashed out at the evil creature with one giant paw, claws racking across the twisted face. The goblin gave a howl of pain and leapt from the wagon. It scampered toward the trees with an uneven gait, as if one leg was shorter than the other. That was one haint down—one to go. I wasn't sure which haint was worse, to tell you the truth. I glared at the black panther and it glared back at me for a terrifying moment. Then it spoke.

"I'll thank you, Joe Cooper, to listen to me when I tell you to stay home at night," the panther said. "I ain't rescuing you from that goblin a second time, do you hear? "

Joe's mouth fell open. "Mattie?" he gasped.

The black panther swished her tail, leapt from the wagon, and vanished in the direction of the Cooper cabin. Without any prompting, Old Nellie followed the panther down the lane at a trot while I stared at Joe in shock.

"My Mattie is a witch?" Joe said. He looked gob-smacked.

"Your Mattie just saved your bacon," I said. "Twice! That goblin must have been stalking you on your way to watch the checker game. It got two of us fer the price of one on the way back. Thank your lucky stars fer your good wife, Joe Cooper. That's what I'm doing."

I watched the lights from the Cooper cabin grow brighter ahead of us and decided Old Nellie and I would spend the night at the Cooper place. Ain't no way I was going back through

Haint Hollow tonight. Well, not unless Mattie Cooper came along for the ride.

As I stopped in front of the barn, I got a whiff of hot apple pie through the open window of the house. Mattie must have set a pie in the oven to warm when she got home from rescuing her stubborn husband from the goblin. What a woman! *I wonder if she's got a sister*, I thought as Joe and I unhitched Old Nellie and led her into the barn. Joe Cooper was a lucky man!

29

Jack-o'-Lantern

When I was just a young boy living down in Alabama with my grandpappy, he told me about the googly-eyed jack-o'-lantern that bounds across the swamps. Folks walking in the dark swamp at night had best be careful or the jack-o'-lantern will lure them with his light. Folks say that once you've seen the jack-o'-lantern, you get this irresistible impulse to follow him wherever he goes. You follow the light until you fall into bogs or pools of water and drown.

"Tommy," my grandpappy used to say, "the only way to resist the jack-o'-lantern when you see him is to turn your coat and your pockets inside out. That will confuse him and he'll leave you alone. If you're not wearing a coat, then you should carry a new knife that's never cut wood. Like many evil creatures, the jack-o'-lantern doesn't like newly forged steel, and he'll keep away."

"Grandpappy, where'd the jack-o'-lantern come from?" I asked him once.

"Well now," said my grandpappy, "I hear tell that Jack was once a man who wanted power and riches. One night he went to the crossroads at midnight, and he made a deal with the devil.

JACK-O'-LANTERN

If the devil made him rich and famous, then in seven years Jack would give the devil his soul.

"The devil was mighty pleased with this agreement. He gave Jack just what he wanted. Jack grew rich and famous, and he married a beautiful girl and was as happy as could be for seven years.

"Then one night the devil came to claim Jack's soul. Now Jack had had seven years to figure out how to weasel out of his bargain with the devil, and he was prepared. He had tacked the sole of an old shoe over his front door.

"On the night the devil showed up, Jack acted as if he was all set to keep his part of the bargain, that is, to turn over his soul and accompany the devil to hell. But suddenly Jack smacked his forehead with his hand and said, 'Wait! I thought if I hid my soul you wouldn't be able to find me. But now that you have, I might as well bring it along.'

"The devil was annoyed with Jack for hiding his soul. 'Where is it?' he asked, not realizing this was a trick.

'Over the door,' said Jack, pointing up at the sole of the old shoe.

"When the devil stood up on a chair and reached for the sole, Jack jumped up quick with a hammer and some nails and nailed the devil's hand to the doorpost.

"'Aiiii!' yelled the devil as Jack slipped the chair out from under his feet. 'Get me down from here!'

"'Sorry, Devil, but you're stuck up there,' said Jack.

"'What do you want from me?' asked the devil.

"'I want my freedom.'

"'We made a bargain,' the devil said, swinging to and fro from his stuck hand.

"'And I nailed you to my doorpost. So what will it be?' asked Jack.

"'All right then,' said the devil. 'You've got your freedom.'

"My, but the devil was grumpy at having been tricked by Jack. Jack got the devil down from the doorpost, and the devil stomped away. And Jack lived to a ripe old age with his beautiful wife and his fine sons and his nice house.

"But when Jack died and went up to heaven, those angels in charge of them pearly gates said, 'You can't come in here, Jack. You struck a bargain with the devil. You'd best be getting on to hell.'

"No matter how Jack argued with the angels, they wouldn't let him into heaven. So finally Jack went down to hell to see the devil. Jack was mighty scared to visit hell, seeing as he tricked the devil so bad during his lifetime.

"Well, Jack knocked on the other gates—the bad ones—and the devil looked out at him.

"'Who's there?' asked the devil, even though the devil sure enough knew it was Jack.

"'It's your old friend Jack,' said Jack.

"'I don't have a friend Jack,' said the devil. 'My friend Jack tricked me and we're not friends anymore.'

"'Come on, devil, let me in,' said Jack. 'I've got no place else to go. They won't let me into heaven.'

"'You don't belong in heaven,' said the devil. 'And you don't belong here either.'

"'Go away and don't come back here,' said the devil. 'You're too smart for hell.'

"'Where will I go? And how will I see in the darkness?' Jack asked desperately.

"The devil threw a chunk of brimstone at Jack. 'Use this to see. I don't care where you go, as long as it isn't here.'

"Well now, Jack didn't have any place else to go. He wasn't allowed in heaven and he wasn't welcome in hell. He bitterly regretted the trick he had played on the devil, but it was too late. So Jack picked up the chunk of brimstone and came back to earth.

"He put the brimstone into an old lantern he found to keep it from blowing out in the wind and used it to light his way through the dark marshes and swamps where he preferred to walk. From that day to this, a bitter and angry jack-o'-lantern wanders the earth, luring people into the swamps and mud holes. Jack's taking out his vengeance on us poor sinners because no one will let him into heaven or hell."

My grandpappy and I sat in silence for a moment after he finished the story. Then my grandpappy looked at me and said, "And that, Johnny, is why you should always carry a new knife when you're walking through the swamp. The jack-o'-lantern doesn't like newly forged steel, so he stays away."

And that's why I always do.

30

Witch Dance

NATCHEZ TRACE, HOUSTON, MS

Thomas was a rascal of a fellow who would rather drink and dance than go to church, but he was a favorite with the ladies, being tall and handsome. Thomas went to all the social events

WITCH DANCE

and was very popular. Still, the minister shook his head over his behavior, fearing for his immortal soul if he kept up his rascally ways.

One fine night Thomas squired a pretty young lady to a town supper. He was in high spirits, for the local ladies had made a fine dinner, and his partner had given him a kiss on the cheek as they entered the building. The only low point came when the minister took him aside for a few moments to talk about his immortal soul and the mending of his ways. Thomas shook him off, but it soured his mood.

After he walked his new young lady home, Thomas dropped by the tavern to have a few drinks. Three old-timers were there, drinking ale and discussing the comings and going on the Natchez Trace.

"You wouldn't catch me near Witch Dance for any money," one bearded fellow slurred into Tom's ear. "Them witches, they feast and dance all night there."

"I hear the grass withers under their feet as they dance, never to grow again," said a wide-eyed local farmer. "I've seen the scorched places with my own eyes."

"They do all kinds of evil ceremonies at night," a third fellow claimed, "calling on the devil and raising demons and such. If'n you get caught by one of their demons, you have to dance until sunrise, or you'll lose your soul."

"That's hogwash," Thomas said. "There's no such thing as witches. It's probably just church folks having a party back in the woods where the minister won't see them."

The old-timers shook their heads at this statement, but nothing they said would convince Thomas that witches were real.

It was close to midnight when Thomas staggered out of the bar. Feeling defiant and reckless, he decided to take the Natchez Trace home so he could see for himself what went on at Witch Dance. He bumbled his way down the Trace, tripping more than once over a root or a sapling along the way. He excused himself politely each time, raising his cap and bowing toward the offended vegetation.

As Thomas neared the scorched spots where the evil ones were said to lurk, he heard the sound of a fiddle floating on the breeze. A light appeared among the trees, and he could hear laughter and the sound of feet shuffling in a dance.

Oh ho, he said to himself. *It seems that I was right. Some of the so-called righteous townsfolk have got themselves up a moonlight dance. The minister should see this. After hearing the sacrilegious music they're playing, he won't be so quick to tell me I'm shaming the town.*

Thomas pushed his way through the thicket, eager to see whom he had caught making merry at Witch Dance. A moment later he found himself on the edge of a clearing. Torches flared on every side, and before him was a joyous crowd milling about, black capes swirling in the midnight breeze. They were dancing in a spirited manner quite unlike any he had ever seen.

Now, Thomas dearly enjoyed a good dance, and this one was better than the best of its kind. His toes tapped to the cheery fiddle tune as he gazed about in wonder. Then he gave a delighted laugh and strode boldly toward the ring of dancers. He offered them an elaborate bow, and they greeted him with a friendly shout.

"Welcome, Thomas. We've been expecting you," a voice called from within the ring of merry people.

A girl with laughing black eyes and rosy-red lips stood in the center of the circle. She eyed Thomas mischievously and twitched her skirt, allowing him to catch a glimpse of her pretty ankles. The invitation in her eyes and her flirtatious sidelong glance were all the incentive Thomas needed to sweep her into a dance. Thomas whirled her about in the wildest dance he had ever led. He seemed to be floating in the air, so light were his heels and so dashing his moves.

Soon an admiring ring had formed around Thomas and his partner, inciting him to new heights and marvelous feats of skill. The fiddle seemed to put lightning in his heels; he could make no wrong move this night. He swung his partner around, and then Thomas gave a mighty leap and a whirl, cracking his heels together. As he came to the ground, he noticed that his partner, who was dancing suggestively toward him, had changed. She looked older; her face had grown longer, and her eyes were dark and hard. Thomas twirled again, and now when he came face-to-face with his partner, he saw with dismay that she had transformed completely. Her form was lank and twisted, her hair wild and disarrayed, her teeth yellow and pointed, and her green eyes full of wickedness and glee.

In that moment Thomas realized that he was in the company of the witches whose ceremonies regularly scorched the earth in this spot. And his partner was the demon they had summoned!

His partner gave him a twisted smile as they joined hands, and the faces in the crowd were no longer noble, though they were still merry. Thomas was trembling with such fear that his legs would barely hold him. But he knew that if he stopped dancing now, his fate would be sealed. If this dance ended before sunrise, the demon would claim his soul for all eternity. It was dance or die.

Thomas threw off his coat and tie and settled into a steady jig, fancy antics forgotten. The moon was setting over the trees, but it was at least two more hours until sunrise. He had to hold out that long. His partner giggled happily and tried to snuggle up to him, but he danced away from her. He could not escape the others so easily. Each way he turned, another gleaming pair of evil eyes or a twisted face watched him. Several witches and warlocks raised their glasses to him in a threatening toast.

By this time Thomas was in agony. His muscles burned and his body was shaking with fatigue. *I must keep dancing*, he told himself, urging himself on. No one else was dancing now. They were all watching him hungrily. The clearing was silent except for the obscenely merry sound of the fiddle.

Suddenly a cramp caught Thomas in the calf. He doubled over in agony, and his onetime partner shouted with glee. She loomed above him, and a whiff of sulfur choked him. "God save me," shouted Thomas, tumbling onto his back.

At the name of God, there came a sudden hissing sound. Thomas heard growls and curses and had a brief vision of cloaked figures scurrying away. The demon, who was hanging greedily over him, burst into flames. The stink of sulfur and the blazing flames overwhelmed him, and Thomas knew no more.

He woke at daybreak. He was lying in the dirt of an overgrown clearing, his coat and his tie next to him. His head pounded fiercely.

"Lord, what a hangover," he moaned, pushing himself up. "And what a terrible dream."

His jackknife fell out of his pocket as he spoke. He bent painfully to pick it up, then immediately dropped it with a terrified gasp. The face of the pretty girl with whom he had danced was etched on the handle. Kneeling down in the dirt, he picked up the knife again. Yes, it was the girl. Slowly he turned the knife over. On the other side was the picture of the demon as she'd looked right before he blacked out.

Feeling sick and feverish, Thomas thrust the knife into his pocket, grabbed his things, and stumbled his way home. He lay in bed for a month with fever. When his health returned, Thomas immediately joined the church, married his pretty partner from the town supper, forsook all worldly entertainments, and never drank anything stronger than tea. The minister was delighted that Thomas had taken his speech to heart, and ever afterward claimed credit for Thomas's reformation. The only folks who knew the truth were the three old-timers at the tavern, but they kept it quiet out of respect for Thomas's reformation.

Resources

Adams, Charles J., III. *Coal Country Ghosts, Legends, and Lore.* Reading, PA: Exeter House Books, 2004.

Adams, Charles J., III, and David J. Seibold. *Pocono Ghosts, Legends and Lore, Book Two.* Reading, PA: Exeter House Books, 1995.

Alan, Ian. *Georgia Ghosts: They Are Among Us.* Birmingham, AL: Sweetwater Press. Produced by Cliff Road Books, 2005.

———. *Virginia Ghosts: They Are Among Us.* Raleigh, NC: Sweetwater Press, 2005.

Alexander, Kathy. *The Witch Dance of the Natchez Trace, Mississippi.* Warsaw, MO: Legends of America, 2023. https://www.legendsofamerica.com/ms-witchdance.

Appalachian Magazine. *Mountain Superstitions, Ghost Stories & Haint Tales.* Charleston, WV: Stately Ties Media, 2018.

Asfar, Dan. *Ghost Stories of Pennsylvania.* Alberta, Canada: Ghost House Books, 2002.

———. *Ghost Stories of Virginia.* Auburn, WA: Lone Pine Publishing, Inc., 2006.

Aswell, James R., et al. *God Bless the Devil: Liar's Bench Tales.* Chapel Hill: The University of North Carolina Press, 1940.

Bahr, Jeff, Troy Taylor, and Loren Coleman. *Weird Virginia.* New York: Sterling Publishing Co., Inc., 2007.

Baldwin, Juanitta. *Smoky Mountain Ghostlore.* Kodak, TN: Suntop Press, 2005.

Barber, Christina A. *Spirits of Georgia's Southern Crescent.* Atglen, PA: Schiffer Publishing, Ltd., 2008.

Barden, Thomas E. *Virginia Folk Legends.* Charlottesville: University Press of Virginia, 1991.

Barefoot, Daniel W. *Haints of the Hills.* Winston-Salem, NC: John F. Blair, Publishers, 2002.

Bender, William N. *Haunted Atlanta and Beyond.* Athens, GA: Hill Street Press, 2005.

Bolton, W. Lewis. *Smoky Mountain Jack Tales of Winter and Old Christmas.* Bloomington, IN: Xlibris, 2015.

Botkin, B. A., ed. *A Treasury of American Folklore.* New York: Crown Publishers, 1944.

———. *A Treasury of New England Folklore.* New York: Crown Publishers, 1965.

———. *A Treasury of Southern Folklore.* New York: Crown Publishers, 1949.

Boyanoski, John. *Ghosts of Upstate South Carolina.* Mountville, PA: Shelor & Son Publishing, 2006.

———. *More Ghosts of Upstate South Carolina.* Mountville, PA: Shelor & Son Publishing, 2008.

Brewer, J. Mason. *American Negro Folklore.* Chicago: Quadrangle Books, 1972.

Brown, Alan. *Haunted Tennessee.* Mechanicsburg, PA: Stackpole Books, 2009.

———. *Stories from the Haunted South.* Jackson: University of Mississippi Press, 2004.

Brown, John N. "History of the Bell Witch." In *Ghosts & Spirits of Tennessee,* 2002. http//johnsrealmonline.com/paranormal/bellwitch/adams.

Boyle, Virginia Frazer. *Devil Tales: Black Americana Folk-Lore.* New York: Harper & Brothers Publishers, 1900.

Buxton, Geordie. *Haunted Plantations.* Charleston, SC: Arcadia Publishing, 2007.

Caperton, Helena Lefroy. *Legends of Virginia.* Richmond, VA: Garrett & Massie, Inc., 1950.

Chase, Richard. *Grandfather Tales.* New York: Houghton Mifflin Company, 1948.

Christian, Reese. *Ghosts of Atlanta.* Charleston, SC: Haunted America, 2008.

Cooper, Horton. *North Carolina Mountain Folklore and Miscellany.* Murfreesboro, NC: Johnson Publishing, 1972.

Coffin, T. P., and H. Cohen. *Folklore in America.* New York: Doubleday and AMP, 1966.

———. *Folklore from the Working Folk of America.* New York: Anchor Press/Doubleday, 1973.

Cohen, Daniel, and Susan Cohen. *Hauntings and Horrors.* New York: Dutton Children's Books, 2002.

Coleman, Christopher K. *Ghosts and Haunts of Tennessee.* Winston-Salem, NC: John F. Blair, Publisher, 2011.

———. *Ghosts and Haunts of the Civil War.* Nashville, TN: Rutledge Hill Press, 1999.

Cox, John Harrington. "Negro Tales from West Virginia," *Journal of American Folklore* 47, no. 186, 1934.

Davis, Donald. *Southern Jack Tales.* Atlanta, GA: August House, Inc., 1992.

Davis, M. L. M. *Journal of American Folklore* 17, No. 70. Boston: Houghton Mifflin, 1905.

Dinan, Kim. *Mothman and the Flatwoods Monster: Bigfoot, Brown Mountain Lights, and the Bell Witch.* Charlottesville, VA: Blue Ridge Outdoors, 2018. https://www.blueridgeoutdoors.com/features/appalachian-legends.

Dolgner, Beth. *Georgia Spirits and Specters.* Atglen, PA: Schiffer Publishing Ltd., 2009.

Dorson, R. M. *America in Legend.* New York: Pantheon Books, 1973.

Duffey, Barbara. *Banshees, Bugles and Belles: True Ghost Stories of Georgia.* Berryville, VA: Rockbridge Publishing Company, 1995.

Duncan, Barbara R., ed. *The Origin of the Milky Way & Other Living Stories of the Cherokee.* Chapel Hill: The University of North Carolina Press, 2008.

Editors of Life. *The Treasury of American Folklore.* New York: Time, 1961.

Flanagan, J. T., and A. P. Hudson. *The American Folk Reader.* New York: A. S. Barnes, 1958.

Floyd, Blanche W. *Ghostly Tales & Legends along the Grand Strand of South Carolina.* Winston-Salem, NC: Bandit Books, 2002.

Foxfire Students. *Boogers, Witches, and Haints: Appalachian Ghost Stories.* New York: Anchor Books, 2011.

Gainer, Patrick W. *Witches, Ghosts and Signs: Folklore of the Southern Appalachians.* Morgantown: West Virginia University Press, 2008.

Georgia Writers' Project. *Drums and Shadows.* Los Angeles: Indo-European Publishing, 2010.

Gethard, Chris. *Weird New York.* New York: Sterling Publishing Co., Inc., 2005.

"Ghost Stories." *The Plain Dealer,* Cleveland, OH. December 16, 1894.

Gibbons, Faye. *Hook Night Moon.* New York: Morrow Junior Books, 1997.

Guy, Joe. *The Hidden History of East Tennessee.* Charleston, SC: The History Press, 2008.

———. *The Hidden History of Southeast Tennessee.* Charleston, SC: The History Press, 2011.

Hall, Joseph S. *Smoky Mountain Folks and Their Lore.* Asheville, NC: Gilbert Printing Co, 1960. Published in Cooperation with Great Smoky Mountains Natural History Association.

———. *Yarns and Tales from the Great Smokies.* Asheville, NC: The Cataloochee Press, 1978.

Hardin, John. *The Devil's Tramping Ground and Other North Carolina Mystery Stories.* Chapel Hill: The University of North Carolina Press, 1949.

———. *Tar Heel Ghosts.* Chapel Hill: The University of North Carolina Press, 1954.

Hauck, Dennis William. *Haunted Places: The National Directory.* New York: Penguin Books, 1996.

"He Married a Ghost. Novel Wedding Which Occurred at Cincinnati. Mr. Thorp's Desire Fulfilled." *Kalamazoo Gazette,* Kalamazoo, MI. October 6, 1896.

Hendricks, W. C. *Bundle of Troubles and Other Tarheel Tales.* Durham, NC: Duke University Press, 1943.

Historic Bell Witch Cave. *History & Legend.* Adams, TN: Bellwitchcave. com, 2023. https://www.bellwitchcave.com.

Hudson, Arthur Palmer, and Pete Kyle McCarter. "The Bell Witch of Tennessee and Mississippi." *Journal of American Folklore* 47, no. 183, 1934.

Huskey, James L. 1956. "The Haunted Church House, and Some Tall Tales." [Transcript of audio interview by Joseph Sargent Hall.] *Joseph Sargent Hall Collection, 1937–1973.* Archives of Appalachia (Box 6, Series I-IB). Johnson City: Eastern Tennessee State University.

Jagendorf, M. A. *The Ghost of Peg-Leg Peter and Other Stories of Old New York.* New York: Vanguard Press, Inc, 1965.

Ingram, Martin Van Buren, 1894. *An Authenticated History of the Famous Bell Witch.* http://bellwitch02.tripod.com.

"John Wilkins, Sharpshooter." *The Morning Times,* Washington, DC. March 28, 1897.

Johnson, Tally. *Ghosts of the South Carolina Upcountry.* Charleston, SC: The History Press, 2005.

Jones, Louis C. *Things That Go Bump in the Night.* New York: Hill and Wang, 1959.

Kazek, Kelly. *Forgotten Tales of Tennessee.* Charleston, SC: The History Press, 2011.

Killion, Ronald G., and Charles T. Waller. A Treasury of Georgia Folklore. Marietta, GA: Cherokee Publishing Company, 1972.

Kinney, Pamela K. *Haunted Virginia: Legends, Myths & True Tales.* Atglen, PA: Schiffer Publishing Ltd., 2009.

Klees, Emerson. *Legends and Stories of the Finger Lakes Region.* New York: Friends of the Finger Lakes Publishing, 1995.

———. *More Legends and Stories of the Finger Lakes Region.* New York: Friends of the Finger Lakes Publishing, 1997.

Korson, George, ed. *Pennsylvania Songs and Legends.* Philadelphia: University of Pennsylvania Press, 1949.

Kotarski, Georgiana. *Ghosts of the Southern Tennessee Valley.* Winston-Salem, NC: John F. Blair, 2006.

Leach, M. *The Rainbow Book of American Folk Tales and Legends.* New York: World Publishing, 1958.

Lee, Marguerite Dupont. *Virginia Ghosts.* Berryville, VA: Virginia Book Company, 1966.

Library of Congress Archive of Folk Culture. *Songs and Ballads of the Anthracite Miner* [compact disc]. Washington, DC: Library of Congress, 2000.

Macken, Lynda Lee. *Adirondack Ghosts.* Forked River, NJ: Black Cat Press, 2000.

———. *Adirondack Ghosts II.* Forked River, NJ: Black Cat Press, 2003.

———. *Empire Ghosts.* Forked River, NJ: Black Cat Press, 2004.

Manly, Roger. *Weird Carolinas.* New York: Sterling Publishing, 2007.

Mathes, Hodge. *Tall Tales from Old Smoky.* Johnson City, TN: The Overmountain Press, 1991.

Middler, Harriet Parks. *The Bell Witch of Middle Tennessee.* Clarksville, TN: Leaf Chronicle Publishing Co, 1930.

Miles, Jim, Mark Sceurman, and Mark Moran. *Weird Georgia.* New York: Sterling Publishing Co., Inc., 2006.

"Mirror Shows the Faces of Bodiless Men. Ghostlike Reflections Mystify Visitors in Chillicothe Home." *Cleveland Plain Dealer*, February 24, 1918.

Mitchell, Faith. *Hoodoo Medicine.* Columbia, SC: Summerhouse Press, 1999.

Morris, Jeff, Donna Marsh, and Garett Merk. *Nashville Haunted Handbook.* Cincinnati, OH: Clerisy Press, 2011.

Mott, A. S. *Ghost Stories of America, Vol. II.* Edmonton, AB: Ghost House Books, 2003.

Norman, Michael, and Beth Scott. *Historic Haunted America.* New York: Tor Books, 1995.

Norton, Terry L. *Cherokee Myths and Legends: Thirty Tales Retold.* Jefferson, NC: McFarland & Company, Inc., Publishers, 2014.

O'Rear, Jim. *Tennessee Ghosts*. Atglen, PA: Schiffer Publishing, Ltd., 2009.

Odum, Howard W. *Cold Blue Moon, Black Ulysses Afar Off.* Indianapolis: Bobbs-Merrill, 1931.

Olson, Ted, and Anthony P. Cavender, eds. *A Tennessee Folklore Sampler*. Knoxville: University of Tennessee Press, 2009.

Pinckney, Roger. *Blue Roots*. Orangeburg, SC: Sandlapper Publishing Co., 2003.

Polley, J., ed. *American Folklore and Legend*. New York: Reader's Digest Association, 1978.

Poore, Tammy J. *Ghost Tales & Superstitions of Southern Appalachian Mountains*. Knoxville, TN: Nine Lives Publishing, 2009.

Price, Charles Edwin. *Haints, Witches, and Boogers: Tales from Upper East Tennessee*. Winston-Salem, NC: John F. Blair, Publisher, 1992.

———. *Haunted Tennessee*. Johnson City, TN: The Overmountain Press, 1995.

———. "Is the Bell Witch Watching?" In *Linda Linn's Kentucky Home and Ghost Stories*. http://members.tripod.com/~lindaluelinn /index-57.html.

Prock, Tabitha. *These Haunted Hills*. Kindle edition. Self-published: CreateSpace Independent Publishing Platform, 2011.

Renegar, Michael. *Roadside Revenants and Other North Carolina Ghosts and Legends*. Fairview, NC: Bright Mountain Books, 2005.

Rhodes, Don. *Mysteries and Legends of Georgia*. Guilford, CT: Globe Pequot Press, 2010.

Rhyne, Nancy. *More Tales of the South Carolina Low Country*. Winston-Salem, NC: John F. Blair, Publisher, 1984.

———. *Tales of the South Carolina Low Country*. Winston-Salem, NC: John F. Blair, Publisher, 1982.

Rivers, Michael. *Appalachia Mountain Folklore*. Atglen, PA: Schiffer Publishing, Ltd., 2012.

Roberts, Nancy, *Ghosts of the Carolinas*. Columbia: University of South Carolina Press, 1962.

———. *Ghosts of the Southern Mountains and Appalachia.* Columbia: University of South Carolina Press, 1988.

———. *North Carolina Ghosts and Legends.* Columbia: University of South Carolina Press, 1959.

———. *The Haunted South.* Columbia: University of South Carolina Press, 1988.

———. *South Carolina Ghosts.* Columbia: University of South Carolina Press, 1983.

Rule, Leslie. *Coast to Coast Ghosts.* Kansas City, KS: Andrews McMeel Publishing, 2001.

Russel, Randy, and Janet Barnett. *The Granny Curse and Other Ghosts and Legends from East Tennessee.* Winston-Salem, NC: John F Blair, Publisher, 1999.

San Souci, Robert D. *Short & Shivery: Thirty Chilling Tales.* New York: Yearling, 1987.

Sawyer, Susan. *Myths and Mysteries of Tennessee.* Guilford, CT: Globe Pequot Press, 2013.

Simmons, Shane S. *Legends & Lore of East Tennessee.* Charleston, SC: The History Press, 2016.

Skinner, Charles M. *American Myths and Legends.* Vol. 1. Philadelphia: J. B. Lippincott, 1903.

———. *Myths and Legends of Our Own Land.* Vols. 1–2. Philadelphia: J. B. Lippincott, 1896.

Slimp, Kevin, ed. *Ghostly Places: A Collection of Chilling Stories about Haunted Places from the Newspapers of Tennessee.* Knoxville, TN: Market Square Publishing, 2017.

Smitten, Susan. *Ghost Stories of New York State.* Auburn, WA: Ghost House Books, 2004.

Still, Laura. *A Haunted History of Knoxville.* Asheville, NC: Stony River Media, 2014.

Taylor, L. B., Jr. *The Ghosts of Charlottesville and Lynchburg and Nearby Environs.* Williamsburg, VA: Virginia Ghosts, 1992.

———. *The Ghosts of Virginia,* Vol. I–XIII. Lynchburg, VA: Progress Printing, 1993–2008.

———. *Haunted Virginia*. Mechanicsburg, PA: Stackpole Books, 2009.

Thay, Edrick. *Ghost Stories of North Carolina*. Auburn, WA: Lone Pine Publishing International, 2005.

———. *Ghost Stories of the Old South*. Auburn, WA: Lone Pine Publishing International, 2003.

Thompson, Harold W. *New York State Folktales, Legends, and Ballads*. New York: Dover Publications, Inc., 1939.

Tolnay, Tom. *Spirits of the Adirondack Mountains*. New York: Birch Brook Press, 2001.

Trapani, Beth E., and Charles J. Adams III. *Ghost Stories of Pittsburgh and Allegheny County*. Reading, PA: Exeter House Books, 1994.

Traylor, Ken, and Delas M. House Jr. *Asheville Ghosts and Legends*. Charleston, SC: Haunted America, 2006.

———. *Nashville Ghosts and Legends*. Charleston, SC: Haunted America, 2007.

Tucker, Elizabeth. *Haunted Southern Tier*. Charleston, SC: Haunted America, 2011.

Underwood, Corinna. *Haunted History of Atlanta and North Georgia*. Atglen, PA: Schiffer Publishing, Ltd., 2008.

"Unveiled by Ghosts: How a Tennessee Mystery Was Explain. Thrilling Story Told About a Haunted House." *Kalamazoo Gazette*, Kalamazoo, MI. December 19, 1895.

Walser, Richard. *North Carolina Legends*. Raleigh: Office of Archives and History, North Carolina Department of Cultural History, 1980.

Wangler, Chris. *Ghost Stories of Georgia*. Auburn, WA: Lone Pine Publishing International, Inc., 2006.

Ward, Marshall. "Marshall Ward: Miles Ward ghost story" [Audio Interview.] *Thomas G. Burton-Ambrose N. Manning Collection, 1899–1989*. Archives of Appalachia (Audiotape 55, Series 8). Johnson City: Eastern Tennessee State University, 1969.

White, Newman Ivey, ed. *The Frank C. Brown Collection of North Carolina Folklore*. Durham, NC: Duke University Press, 1958.

Wigginton, Eliot, ed., and his students. *Foxfire 2.* New York: Anchor Books, 1973.

Wigginton, Eliot, ed., and Margie Bennett. *Foxfire 9.* New York: Anchor Books, 1986.

Wilson, Patty A. *Haunted North Carolina.* Mechanicsburg, PA: Stackpole Books, 2009.

———. *The Pennsylvania Ghost Guide, Vol. 1.* Waterfall, PA: Piney Creek Press, 2000.

———. *The Pennsylvania Ghost Guide, Vol. 2.* Waterfall, PA: Piney Creek Press, 2001.

Wincik, Stephanie. *Ghosts of Erie County.* Self-published, 2002.

Windham, Kathryn Tucker. *13 Georgia Ghosts and Jeffery.* Tuscaloosa: University of Alabama Press, 1973.

———. *13 Mississippi Ghosts and Jeffrey.* Tuscaloosa: The University of Alabama Press, 2015.

———. *13 Tennessee Ghosts and Jeffrey.* Tuscaloosa: The University of Alabama Press, 2016.

Winfield, Mason. *Shadows of the Western Door.* Buffalo, NY: Western New York Wares, Inc., 1997.

———. *Spirits of the Great Hill.* Buffalo, NY: Western New York Wares, Inc., 2001.

———. *Haunted Places of Western New York.* Buffalo, NY: Western New York Wares, Inc., 2006.

———. *Ghost Stories from the American Southwest.* Little Rock, AR: August House, Inc., 1991.

Zeple, Terrance. *Best Ghost Tales of North Carolina.* Sarasota, FL: Pineapple Press, 2006.

———. *Best Ghost Tales of South Carolina.* Sarasota, FL: Pineapple Press, 2004.

———. *Lowcountry Voodoo.* Sarasota, FL: Pineapple Press, 2009.

About the Author

S. E. Schlosser has been telling stories since she was a child, when games of "let's pretend" quickly built into full-length stories acted out with friends. A graduate of Houghton College, the Institute of Children's Literature and Rutgers University, she created and

maintains the website AmericanFolklore.net, where she shares a wealth of stories from all fifty states, some dating back to the origins of America. Sandy spends much of her time answering questions from visitors to the site. Many of her favorite emails come from other folklorists who delight in practicing the old tradition of who can tell the tallest tale.

About the Illustrator

Artist **Paul G. Hoffman** trained in painting and printmaking. His first extensive illustration work on assignment was in Egypt, drawing ancient wall reliefs for the University of Chicago. His work graces books of many genres—including children's titles, textbooks, short story collections, natural history volumes, and numerous cookbooks. For *Spooky Appalachia*, he employed a scratchboard technique and an active imagination.

Printed in the USA
CPSIA information can be obtained
at www.ICGtesting.com
CBHW070253230524
8850CB00006B/6